# FRENCH COOKING

Patricia Cook Sinclair
Ruth Knighton Malinowski

WEATHERVANE
BOOKS

# contents

# introduction

French cooking is generally acknowledged as one of the great cuisines of the world, if not the greatest. The French have a passion for food and demand high quality at home and from restaurants. French women take great pride in their cooking and plan carefully to create a harmonious meal. Even the simplest meal is garnished and tastefully presented. Mealtime is family time, when all members gather together to enjoy good food and to socialize.

There are two basic divisions of French cooking: haute cuisine and provincial cooking.

Haute cuisine has developed in France over the past few centuries. Probably the most famous of the chefs involved in the development of these refined and sophisticated dishes was Escoffier, who rose to become one of the world's great chefs. Escoffier, like most chefs, came from the provinces to Paris, to study the art of food preparation.

French provincial cooking is said to have evolved over the past thousand or so years. Recipes are handed down from generation to generation, often with no changes. Each recipe uses the best of the foods, herbs, and wines available in each region or province of France.

While haute cuisine and provincial cooking are interrelated, both may be clearly defined.

Haute cuisine is carefully orchestrated to please all the senses. Appearance, aroma, and flavor are each considered in the presentation of a meal. Flavors are subtle and delicate; individual flavors often cannot be distinguished, blending to form the perfect end result. Haute cuisine usually requires much time and money, using only the finest ingredients, such as truffles and lots of fresh butter and cream. In the preparation of these *grande* dishes many steps are involved. Although each step is simple, each is essential, and omitting or combining procedures results in a less than perfect result. Chefs are taught to blend, balance, and transform basic foods into feasts. Because of the time restrictions of American housewives, most recipes in this book are simplified and do not require an entire day to prepare.

French provincial cooking contrasts greatly with haute cuisine of famous Paris restaurants. In all provinces of France, and the regions within each province, the basic home cooking depends on locally grown vegetables and locally produced or caught meats, poultry, or fish. Most provincial dishes make their own juices in the casserole as they slowly cook. Oftentimes the most famous dishes are the basis of seasonal feasts, prepared when fresh ingredients are at their peak.

*Terrine, daube, ratatouille,* and *cassoulet* are several examples of famous dishes in provincial cooking. No one disputes that *cassoulet* is the traditional dish of Lanquedoc, but many verbal battles have been fought as to which village can claim the original.

Dishes from Normandy are rich in cream and butter from the herds of dairy cattle. Apples are grown locally. In cooking and for drinking, hard apple cider is used, as this province has no native wine.

Any combination recipes from Provence are easily recognized by their generous use of garlic, tomatoes, zucchini, eggplants, parsley, and thyme, all of which flourish in the warm Mediterranean climate.

A meal in France follows a definite pattern. Breakfast is usually only a croissant or bread with fresh butter and cafe au lait. Traditionally, the main meal of the day is served at midday, during which everyone takes about a 2-hour break. In the cities this pattern is disappearing, as workers are unable to return home.

The first course of any meal is the hors d'oeuvre (meaning aside from the main work). This course is usually simple and served cold. It is never omitted and is eaten with a knife and fork.

Many cold vegetable dishes are served as hors d'oeuvres. If not served as a first course, vegetables are served as a garnish for the main course or as a part of the main dish. The French method of preparing a vegetable is to cook it in a large amount of boiling water until tender-crisp. The vegetable is then plunged into cold water to stop cooking and preserve flavor and color. Before serving, the vegetable is reheated with a little butter. Sometimes vegetables such as celery hearts or lettuce are braised, and the liquid is reduced and used as a sauce. Another method of preparation, called glazing, is to cook the vegetable in a little stock with added sugar.

Soups are not generally served during the main meal at midday. They are usually served at supper, as the main course. The rich, creamy soups, such as asparagus soup, are served at great banquets with many courses.

The main course follows the hors d'oeuvres. In France, the most popular beef dish is beef braised with vegetables, called *boeuf a la mode*. Roast spring lamb is a seasonal favorite. Lamb is also served with white beans or as *cassoulet*. Innards (such as liver) are considered delicacies in France and are carefully prepared to be tender and flavorful. Poultry includes chicken, duck, goose, and wild birds. It is sauteed, fricasseed, or roasted and is often flavored with tarragon or lemon. French women purchase chickens whole, not cut-up, and cut it themselves for more flavor. Duck, goose, and wild birds are treated especially to compensate for their extra richness or wild flavor. Fish is freshly caught or purchased. It may be dusted with flour and sauteed in butter, or it may be poached in a court bouillon and served with a sauce.

A green salad follows the main course. The only salad recognized by Frenchmen consists of fresh, crisp greens with a lightly seasoned oil and vinegar dressing. Sometimes a fresh herb may be added to the dressing, especially if it was used in a preceding dish.

Bread is purchased fresh daily, usually at the village bakery. This fresh bread is on the table throughout the entire meal. Butter is not served, except at breakfast. If cheese is served for dessert, bread will be eaten then, too.

Dessert is often fruit and cheese. On special occasions, however, something more elaborate will be served. Most French families purchase pastry from special shops and do not bake their own. Basic to French desserts are the custard cream and sweet pastry dough. Cakes are leavened by eggs, not baking powder, and are about 1½ inches high. Many cakes and pastries are filled with fresh fruits. Dessert may be a light, refreshing finale to a meal or, when special care is taken, the high point of the meal itself.

Wine is accepted as being necessary to the meal. The French do not drink cocktails, but may have an aperitif before a meal. Each region produces wines suited to its own foods, and these wines are the ones most often drunk. White dry wines usually accompany hors d'oeuvres, poultry, and fish. Red wines are served with meats and cheeses. Certain orders of serving are followed: white before red, young before old, and lesser wines before more important ones. Children are served wine, although it is often mixed with water. The choice of wine to serve with a meal depends on individual preferences, but the above guidelines were developed over the years, since these wines usually complement the groups of foods recommended.

Every region of France has its own special cheese. It may be made from cow's, sheep's, or goat's milk, and may be soft or hard, ripened or mild-flavored. The choice of a cheese to serve as dessert usually depends on the wine served with the meal. France has about 400 varieties of cheeses, most of which are unavailable in the United States.

French cheeses can be subdivided into 4 types: semisoft, soft-ripened, cremes, and goat cheeses. Soft cheeses include Cantal, a cheddar-type; *Port du Salut* (Trappist); *St. Paulin*; and *bonbel*. These cheeses are mild-flavored and creamy-textured. Roquefort is a ripened, blue-veined cheese, with a salty, tangy flavor. Brie, Camembert, Port l'Eveque, and Coulommiers are the most famous soft-ripened cheeses. They have an edible rind and, when ripe, a creamy interior. Each has a distinctive flavor and as they become very ripe their flavor becomes stronger.

Creme cheeses are very rich and may have a butter-fat content of 60 percent or more. *Gourmandise,* a double cream, can be purchased with walnut or kirsch flavoring. Triple creams, such as *belletoile,* taste like butter. *Boursin,* also a triple creme, is seasoned with herbs and pepper. *Petits suisses* is a firm cream cheese, less rich than most cheeses.

Goat cheeses are strong-flavored, and as they age their flavor increases. Two of the more famous goat cheeses are *St. Marcellin* and *Montrachet*.

One or possibly two of the above cheeses makes a fine choice for dessert. They should be served with fresh fruits, such as grapes, apples, or pears.

The cuisine of France has developed over many centuries. Patterns set a long time ago are still followed today, although they are slowly changing. A French meal may be simple or extravagant, but it is always carefully planned and meticulously prepared, using only the highest quality foods. Bon appetit!

*quiche lorraine*

# hors d'oeuvres

## cheese, bacon, and onion quiche
*quiche lorraine*

1 single–crust Basic Pastry
   (see Index; do not bake)
6 slices bacon, cut into 2-inch pieces
1 small onion, chopped
3 eggs
½ cup milk
½ cup heavy cream
1 cup shredded Swiss cheese
½ teaspoon salt
$^1/_8$ teaspoon pepper

Line quiche or pie pan with pastry.
Cook bacon until crisp. Drain; place in pie shell.
Sauté onion in bacon fat until lightly browned. Drain off fat. Off heat, stir in the eggs, milk, cream, cheese, and seasonings. Pour into pastry-lined pan.
Bake in preheated 375°F oven 25 minutes or until a knife plunged into the custard comes out clean.
Serve hot, warm, or cold. Makes 4 servings.

# country meat loaf
*terrine*

¾ pound sliced bacon, boiled 10 minutes
1 tablespoon unsweetened butter
1 cup chopped onion
1 pound ground pork
½ pound ground veal
½ pound finely chopped chicken livers
2 cloves garlic, crushed
½ teaspoon salt
¼ teaspoon allspice
⅛ teaspoon ground cloves
⅛ teaspoon ground nutmeg
¼ teaspoon pepper
2 eggs, beaten
½ cup heavy cream
2 tablespoons sherry
½ pound boiled ham, cut into strips ¼ inch thick (optional)
1 bay leaf

Line a 2-quart mold, casserole, or 9 x 5 x 3-inch loaf pan with bacon. Save 3 slices for the top.
Melt butter in small pan; cook onion until tender.
In a 2-quart bowl mix onion, ground meats, liver, seasonings, eggs, cream and sherry. Beat several minutes to lighten. Place ⅓ of mixture into mold. Lay ½ of the ham over meat mixture. Add ⅓ more meat mixture, ham, and finish with meat mixture. Lay 3 bacon strips over loaf; place bay leaf on top. Cover tightly with aluminum foil and a lid. Place in a hot-water bath.
Bake in preheated 350° oven about 1½ to 2 hours. The juices will be clear when loaf is done. Place a weight on top of loaf to press out air. Cool loaf at room temperature. Refrigerate overnight. Unmold and serve loaf chilled. Makes 8 servings.

# oysters rockefeller
*huîtres à la florentine*

2 tablespoons chopped green onion
2 tablespoons chopped celery
3 tablespoons chopped fennel (optional)
3 tablespoons chopped parsley
¼ pound butter
1 cup watercress or spinach
3 tablespoons bread crumbs
3 tablespoons Pernod or anisette
¼ teaspoon salt
⅛ teaspoon white pepper
Dash cayenne
2 dozen oysters on the half shell

Sauté onion, celery, and herbs in 3 tablespoons butter for 3 minutes. Add watercress or spinach; let it wilt. Place this mixture, remaining butter, bread crumbs, liqueur, and seasonings into blender. Blend for 1 minute.
Put 1 tablespoon mixture on each oyster. Place oyster shells on rock-salt beds; dampen the salt slightly.
Bake at 450°F about 4 minutes or until butter is melted and oysters are heated. Makes 4 servings.

# chicken-liver pate
*pâté de foie de volaille*

2 tablespoons butter
½ pound chicken livers
2 eggs, hard-cooked
1 package (3-ounce size) cream cheese, softened
1 tablespoon finely chopped parsley
¾ teaspoon salt
⅛ teaspoon pepper
1 tablespoon cognac

Heat butter in medium frypan. Cook chicken livers, stirring occasionally, over medium heat 10 minutes or until tender. Drain. Chop livers and eggs in food grinder (or in blender, a little at a time). With wooden spoon, work cream cheese until light and fluffy. Mix cheese into liver mixture along with remaining ingredients.
Refrigerate for several hours.
Serve pate with hot toast or crackers. Makes 1¼ cups.

# marinated mushrooms
## champignons marines

1 pound small whole
mushrooms

*marinade*

1 cup chicken broth
1 cup dry white wine
2 tablespoons fresh lemon juice
¼ cup white vinegar
¼ cup vegetable oil

1 stalk celery
1 clove garlic, peeled
¼ teaspoon rosemary
¼ teaspoon marjoram
¼ teaspoon thyme
⅛ teaspoon oregano
1 bay leaf
4 peppercorns
¼ teaspoon salt

Combine all ingredients except mushrooms in a 2-quart saucepan; bring to a boil. Simmer gently 30 minutes. Strain Marinade, pressing juice from vegetables. Return to saucepan. Add mushrooms; simmer for 5 minutes. Cool to room temperature, then chill at least 4 hours, preferably overnight. Makes 4 servings.

# fresh vegetables with green mayonnaise
## crudites à la sauce verte

*green mayonnaise*

¼ teaspoon sugar
½ teaspoon dry mustard
¾ teaspoon salt
1 large (or 2 small) egg yolk
2 tablespoons fresh lemon juice
¾ cup vegetable oil plus ¼ cup
   French olive oil or 1 cup
   vegetable oil

2 tablespoons chopped parsley
1 teaspoon fresh or frozen
   chives
1 teaspoon fresh or dried
   tarragon (optional)

**Fresh vegetables for dipping, such as mushrooms, cherry tomatoes, cauliflower florets, zucchini sticks, green-pepper slices, cucumber slices, carrot sticks.**

Mix sugar, mustard, salt, egg yolk, and 1 tablespoon lemon juice in 1-quart bowl. Using wire whisk, very slowly add oil, a drop at a time, until about ¼ cup is added. Once a thick emulsion has formed, oil can be added 1 teaspoon at a time. When mixture is very thick, add remaining lemon juice. Slowly beat in remaining oil. Add herbs; mix well. Chill.
Arrange chilled vegetables attractively on a large platter, with mayonnaise in the center as a dip. Makes 8 servings.

**Note:** If mayonnaise separates, place 1 teaspoon cold water or an egg yolk in a separate bowl. Slowly beat in mayonnaise. When emulsion is reformed, continue adding oil as above.

# roquefort cheese balls
## amuse-gueuleau

¼ pound Roquefort cheese
3 tablespoons unsalted butter,
   softened
1 tablespoon minced
   green-onion tops

Freshly ground pepper to taste
2 teaspoons brandy
¼ cup bread crumbs
2 tablespoons finely minced
   parsley

Mash cheese in small bowl. Beat in butter to form a smooth paste. Blend in onion, pepper, and brandy. Shape into small balls, about ½ inch in diameter.
Mix crumbs and parsley. Roll balls in crumb mixture. Chill, if made ahead.
Serve cheese balls at room temperature, with crusty French bread. Makes 24 balls, 6 appetizer servings.

# artichoke appetizers
*apértif au artichaut*

2 large artichokes, cooked
   according to basic directions
   (see Index, Boiled Artichokes)
6 ounces cream cheese, softened
½ teaspoon Tabasco sauce
¼ teaspoon garlic powder
¼ teaspoon salt
4 tablespoons half-and-half or
   milk
About ½ pound small shrimp,
   cooked

Gently remove leaves from prepared artichokes. Use leaves that are
firm enough to handle and have a good edible portion.
Beat cream cheese, seasonings, and milk until smooth and creamy.
Place about ½ teaspoon cream cheese on base of each leaf. Garnish
with a shrimp on each leaf.
Arrange leaves on a large, round plate in a sunflower shape. Chill.
Makes about 36.

# artichoke hearts with mushroom filling
*fonds d'artichauts aux champignons*

*mushroom filling*

2 tablespoons butter
1 tablespoon minced shallots
½ pound finely chopped
   mushrooms
¼ teaspoon salt
Dash pepper
⅛ teaspoon tarragon
1 tablespoon flour
2 tablespoons brandy or sherry
½ cup heavy cream
6 artichoke bottoms
   (recipe follows)

Melt butter in small saucepan. Cook shallots several minutes. Add
mushrooms; cook until all liquid is evaporated. Add seasonings; stir
in flour. Add brandy and cream; heat until thickened.
Place about 2 tablespoons filling on each artichoke bottom. Place
filled bottoms in greased casserole; cover.
Heat for 10 to 15 minutes in preheated 300°F oven. Serve hot.
Makes 6 servings.

# boiled artichokes
*artichauts au naturel*

6 artichokes
6 quarts water
3 tablespoons salt
Hollandaise Sauce (see Index)
   or melted butter

Cut off artichoke stalks, pull off hard outer leaves, and trim off
points of remaining leaves with scissors. Cut off about ¼ of the
top, which removes many thorny pointed leaves. Place artichokes in
boiling salted water; boil about 45 minutes or until the base is
tender but not mushy. Drain upside down.
Before serving, remove choke or hairy growth in center by opening
top leaves and pulling out tender center or cone in one piece. Below
this cone is the choke. Scrape off with a spoon to expose the tender
artichoke heart. Discard choke. Replace cone upside down in
center. Fill with Hollandaise Sauce, or serve butter separately.
Pull off each leaf, beginning at bottom. Dunk base of leaf in sauce;
pull between the teeth to scrape off the tender flesh. Discard
remainder of leaf. Continue this way until all leaves are eaten.
Discard cone, cut base into wedges, and dip into remaining sauce.
Makes 6 servings.

# salads and dressings

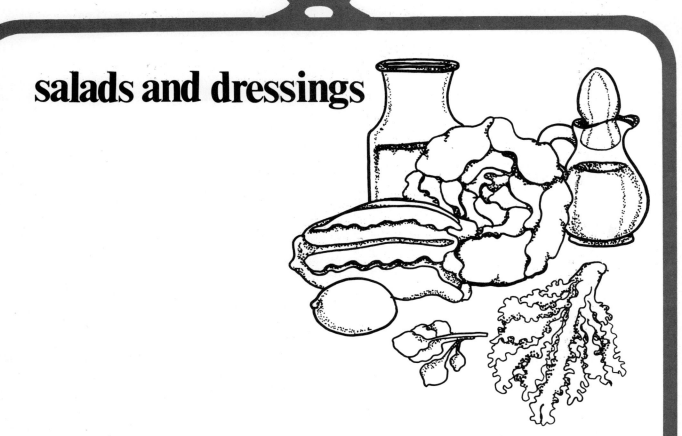

## green salad
### *salade verte*

The only salad recognized in France is a mixture of crisp, dry greens, served with a light dressing.

**2 quarts lettuce leaves, such as romaine, escarole, Bibb, or Boston, washed, dried, and chilled**

*salad dressing*

⅔ **cup vegetable oil**
⅓ **cup fresh lemon juice**
½ **teaspoon sugar**
¼ **teaspoon pepper**
½ **teaspoon salt**
**1 clove garlic, crushed (optional)**
¼ **teaspoon dry mustard**

Place lettuce in large wooden serving bowl.
Mix remaining ingredients for salad dressing.
A very light flavor of garlic can be obtained by rubbing salad bowl with cut garlic clove.
Pour dressing over lettuce; toss to coat leaves. Use only enough dressing to coat leaves lightly. Serve at once. Makes 8 servings.

# nicoise salad
*salade niçoise*

A delicious picnic dish in France or the United States.

**8 small potatoes, cooked and
  still hot**
**½ cup finely chopped onion**
**1 pound fresh green beans,
  cooked and still hot**

*salad dressing*

**¾ cup vegetable oil**
**⅓ cup red wine vinegar**
**¼ teaspoon salt**
**⅛ teaspoon pepper**
**¼ teaspoon dry mustard**

**4 tomatoes, peeled and
  quartered**
**4 hard-cooked eggs, quartered**
**16 large ripe olives**
**1 small can anchovy fillets
  (optional)**
**2 lemons, cut into wedges**
**1 or 2 7-ounce cans tuna,
  drained**

Slice potatoes into large bowl with a cover. Add onion and green beans.
Mix oil, vinegar, salt, pepper, and mustard.
Pour ⅓ cup dressing over hot vegetables. Cover; let cool to room temperature. Refrigerate for several hours.
To serve salad, place potatoes and green beans on large platter. Carefully arrange tomatoes, eggs, olives, anchovies, lemons, and tuna on platter. Serve with dressing separate. Makes 4 servings.

# basic
# salad dressing
*sauce vinaigrette de salade*

This dressing keeps well.

**¾ cup olive oil**
**¼ cup red wine vinegar**
**1 teaspoon salt**
**1 teaspoon sugar (optional)**
**½ teaspoon dry mustard**
**⅛ teaspoon cayenne pepper**

Combine all ingredients; shake well (use a jar with a lid). Makes 1 cup.

## sherry bisque
*bisque de l'xérèx*

**1 small ham hock**
**¾ cup split green peas**
**1 bay leaf**
**6 cups beef broth**
**6 slices bacon, diced**
**¾ cup chopped onion**
**1 stalk celery, diced**
**3 tablespoons flour**
**1 8-ounce can tomato puree**
**1 cup chicken broth**
**⅓ cup sherry**
**¼ cup butter**
**Freshly ground pepper to taste**

Place ham hock, split peas, bay leaf, and 4 cups beef broth into 4-quart saucepan. Bring to a boil, reduce heat, and simmer.
Sauté bacon in frypan until fat is rendered. Add onion and celery; cook until tender. Stir in flour; mix to blend. Add remaining 2 cups beef broth; cook until slightly thickened. Add onion mixture to split-pea mixture; continue to cook until split peas are soft, about 1½ hours.
When done, remove ham hock. Puree mixture in blender or food mill. Add tomato puree, chicken broth, and sherry. Add butter and pepper; stir until melted.
Strain soup, if desired, before serving. Makes 8 to 12 servings.

*onion soup*

# onion soup
*soupe à l'oignon*

4 large onions, thinly sliced
1 tablespoon butter
1 tablespoon vegetable oil
¼ teaspoon sugar
2 tablespoons flour
6 cups beef broth
¼ cup dry white wine or
  vermouth

Salt and pepper to taste
4 slices French bread, cut ½
  inch thick
2 teaspoons vegetable oil
1 clove garlic, peeled and cut
2 tablespoons cognac
1 cup grated Swiss cheese

In covered 4-quart saucepan or Dutch oven cook onions slowly with
butter and oil for 15 minutes. Stir occasionally. Uncover; increase
heat to moderate. Add sugar; sauté onions, stirring frequently,
about 30 minutes or until onions turn golden brown. Sprinkle
onions with flour; stir over heat for 2 to 3 minutes. Blend in hot
broth and wine; adjust seasonings. Simmer, partially covered, for 1
hour.
Meanwhile, place bread slices in 350°F oven 30 minutes or until
lightly toasted. Halfway through the baking, baste each slice with
½ teaspoon oil, and rub with cut garlic clove.
Before serving, add cognac and divide soup into ovenproof bowls
or casseroles. Sprinkle ½ cup cheese in soup. Float slices of French
bread on top of soup; sprinkle with rest of cheese.
Bake in preheated 325°F oven 15 to 20 minutes, until hot, then set
under broiler for 2 to 3 minutes, until cheese is golden brown.
Serve immediately. Makes 4 servings.

# potato soup
## vichyssoise

3 to 4 leeks or green onions
1 medium onion, chopped
2 tablespoons butter
2 large potatoes, peeled and diced
½ teaspoon salt

3 cups chicken broth
1 cup milk
1½ cups heavy cream
1 drop Tabasco sauce
1 tablespoon minced parsley or chives

Thoroughly clean leeks or onions, halve lengthwise, and cut into thin slices.

Heat butter. Add leeks or onions; cook until transparent. Add potatoes, salt, and chicken broth. Simmer mixture 35 minutes. Puree in blender or food mill; reheat. Pour in milk and 1 cup cream. Heat and stir until well-blended, but do not boil. Season with Tabasco sauce. Chill mixture.

Beat ½ cup cream until stiff; fold into soup. Adjust seasonings. Serve soup garnished with chopped chives or parsley. Makes 4 servings.

*fish soup normandy*

14

# consommé
*consummé*

½ cup cold water
4 egg whites
1 quart Basic Stock, cold (see Index)
1 teaspoon salt

⅛ teaspoon pepper
Brown food coloring
1 tablespoon Madeira
1 tablespoon cognac

Put water and egg whites into medium saucepan; beat to a foam. Add cold stock, salt, and pepper; heat to a boil. Just as mixture starts to boil, reduce heat and simmer for 8 to 10 minutes. Pour liquid through wet cheesecloth. Do not break up egg whites. After straining, color with food coloring if beef stock is used. (Chicken consommé is not colored.) Flavor with Madeira and cognac. Serve consommé plain or with garnish. Makes 6 servings.

# fish soup normandy
*soupe de poisson normande*

*fish stock*

½ pound fish (heads, bones, or trimmings)
4 cups hot beef bouillon
Juice of ½ lemon
1 small onion, sliced
1 stalk celery, sliced
1 carrot, sliced

*fish dumplings*

¾ pound cooked white fish (cod, haddock, etc.)
¼ teaspoon salt
⅛ teaspoon white pepper
1 tablespoon butter
1 egg
3 sprigs parsley, finely chopped
2 teaspoons lemon juice
3 tablespoons packaged bread crumbs

*soup ingredients*

3 tablespoons vegetable oil
1 medium onion, sliced
5 carrots, sliced into ½ inch lengths
1 stalk celery, sliced into ½ inch lengths
2 sprigs parsley
2 cups hot beef broth
2 tablespoons tomato paste
1 4-ounce can sliced mushrooms, drained
3 small tomatoes, peeled and quartered
1 teaspoon curry powder
1 green pepper, sliced
1 4½-ounce can shrimp, deveined and drained
¾ cup white wine
Salt to taste
Dash cayenne pepper
Dash garlic powder
1 sprig parsley, chopped

Clean fish, trimming well. Place into large saucepan. Add bouillon, lemon juice, onion, celery, and carrot. Simmer over low heat 1 hour. Strain.
To prepare Fish Dumplings, put fish through meat grinder (fine blade). Season with salt and pepper. Blend in butter and egg. Add parsley, lemon juice, and bread crumbs. Mix well; set aside.
In large Dutch oven or saucepan, heat oil, add onion, carrots, celery, and parsley; while stirring constantly, cook until slightly browned. Gradually add beef broth. Cover; simmer over low heat 20 minutes. Add Fish Stock, tomato paste, mushrooms, tomatoes, curry powder, and green pepper. Continue simmering for 10 minutes.
Moisten your hands; shape Fish Dumplings. Drop them into soup. Add shrimp; simmer for 15 minutes more. Pour in wine. Season to taste with salt, cayenne pepper, and garlic powder. Stir in chopped parsley. Serve. Makes 6 servings.

# asparagus soup
*potage crème
d'asperges vertes*

30 stalks asparagus (about 2 pounds)
4 quarts water
1 tablespoon salt
¼ cup minced onion
¼ cup minced parsley
1 teaspoon ground coriander
2 tablespoons butter
1 tablespoon flour
2 cups chicken broth, heated
½ cup heavy cream
1 tablespoon lemon juice
½ teaspoon salt
¼ teaspoon white pepper

Peel asparagus with potato peeler; trim tough ends. Tie together in 3 bunches; simmer in large pot of salted water until just tender. Lift bundles out; place in sink of cold water. When cool, drain on paper towels. Cut tips from stalks; reserve. Cut stalks into 1-inch pieces; reserve.
In medium saucepan, sauté onion and parsley with coriander and butter until vegetables are softened. Stir in flour; cook for 3 minutes. Remove pan from heat; stir in heated broth. Simmer mixture 5 minutes. Add reserved asparagus stalks. Puree mixture in blender or food mill until smooth. Do this by batches. Return puree to saucepan; stir in cream and reserved asparagus tips; heat through. Stir in lemon juice. Add salt and pepper; adjust seasonings to taste.
Serve soup hot or chilled. Makes 6 servings.

# cream of lettuce soup
*potage crème de laitues*

¼ cup butter
1 leek or green onion, chopped
½ cup chopped onion
1 quart shredded lettuce*
4 tablespoons flour
1 tablespoon chopped parsley
½ teaspoon salt
⅛ teaspoon nutmeg
6 cups chicken broth
2 egg yolks
½ cup heavy cream
Lettuce and parsley for garnish

Melt the butter in 3-quart saucepan. Add leek or onion; sauté until tender. Add lettuce; cover; simmer for 5 minutes. Stir in flour. Add parsley and seasonings and chicken broth. Simmer gently 30 minutes. Puree soup in blender.
Mix egg yolks and cream in small bowl. Stir in ¼ cup hot soup. Gradually add egg mixture to hot soup, stirring constantly. Heat gently several minutes, until soup thickens.
Garnish soup with shredded lettuce and parsley. Makes 8 servings.

*Use Boston Bibb or romaine lettuce for best flavor. Do not use iceberg (head) lettuce.

# sauces and stocks

## vinegar sauce
*sauce vinaigrette*

Excellent on salads or for marinades. With capers added, this sauce is particularly good on boiled chicken, fish, or vegetables.

**½ cup fresh chopped herbs
(chervil, tarragon, parsley,
chives)**
**1 teaspoon capers (optional)**
**6 tablespoons vegetable oil**
**2 tablespoons white wine vinegar**
**½ teaspoon salt**
**1/8 teaspoon white pepper**
**Pinch of sugar**

Mince herbs and capers until very fine.
Blend oil with vinegar, salt, pepper, and sugar. Stir in herbs and capers. Store for several hours to age. Makes about ¾ cup.

# basic stock
*fond de cuisine simple*

3 pounds beef bones
2 pounds lean beef
4 quarts water
4 green onions with tops
1 large onion, studded with
  10 cloves
1 celery stalk and leaves
2 carrots

Place bones and beef in large baking pan. Bake at 400°F about an hour. Remove from pan; place in large pot.

Pour off fat from baking pan. Add ½ cup water to pan; scrape up brown particles from pan bottom. Pour into pot. Add remaining ingredients. Slowly bring to a boil. Skim off the impurities which collect on the top of the liquid. Partially cover; simmer for 3 to 4 hours.

Remove meat and vegetables. Strain stock through wet cheesecloth. Chill. Remove fat before using. Makes about 2 quarts.

*Note:* To make chicken stock, substitute 2 medium fryers for beef bones and meat.

# basic brown sauce
*sauce brune*

2 onions, diced
2 carrots, diced
4 tablespoons butter
1 tablespoon sugar
¼ cup flour
2 cups beef bouillon
2 cups water
1 clove garlic, minced
2 sprigs parsley
1 bay leaf
⅛ teaspoon thyme
1 tablespoon tomato paste
¼ teaspoon salt
⅛ teaspoon pepper
1 tablespoon Madeira
2 tablespoons cognac

Sauté onions and carrots in butter for 20 minutes. Add sugar; increase heat to brown vegetables. Cook about 10 minutes, stirring very often. Do not let vegetables burn. Stir in flour; cook about 3 minutes. Add bouillon, water, garlic, parsley, bay leaf, thyme, tomato paste, salt and pepper. Bring to a boil while stirring.

Reduce heat; partially cover; simmer about 1¼ hours.

Strain sauce into clean pan; discard vegetables. After cooling, sauce may be frozen at this point.

Just before serving, add Madeira and cognac. Makes 2 cups.

# bearnaise sauce
*sauce bearnaise*

¼ cup white vinegar
¼ cup dry white wine
1 tablespoon minced green
  onion
1 teaspoon dried tarragon
3 peppercorns
3 egg yolks
1 tablespoon warm water
½ cup butter
¼ teaspoon salt

Boil vinegar, wine, onion, tarragon, and peppercorns in small saucepan until liquid has reduced to 2 tablespoons. Pour liquid through fine sieve.

In top of double boiler, over just simmering water, blend egg yolks and warm water until creamy. Bottom of double boiler should not touch water.

Melt butter over low heat; add by ½ teaspoons to yolk mixture, beating well with a wire whip after each addition. (Set bottom of pan in a cold-water bath if eggs start to look like scrambled eggs.) After some butter has been added, up to 1 teaspoon of butter can be added at one time. Leave the white residue in bottom of butter pan. After butter is added, stir in vinegar mixture and salt. Makes about ¾ cup.

# hollandaise sauce
## sauce hollandaise

3 egg yolks
2 tablespoons lemon juice
¼ teaspoon salt
⅛ teaspoon white pepper
½ cup butter

Place egg yolks, lemon juice, salt, and pepper in blender.
Carefully melt butter in small pan; heat to foaming.
Blend yolk mixture at top speed 3 seconds. Remove center of cover.
Pour in hot butter *by droplets* at first, then in a thin stream. Omit the milky residue at bottom of pan. Adjust seasonings, if desired.
Set jar in lukewarm water until ready to use. Reheating usually causes curdling, so prepare close to serving time. Makes ¾ cup.

# basic aspic
## gelée

1 envelope unflavored gelatin
1¼ cups cold water
1 cup canned beef bouillon
1 tablespoon lemon juice
1 tablespoon port
1 tablespoon cognac

Soften gelatin in ¼ cup cold water.
Combine bouillon and 1 cup cold water in small saucepan; bring to a boil. Add softened gelatin; stir until dissolved. Remove from heat. Stir in lemon juice, port, and cognac.
Use aspic for congealed molds or glazes. Makes 2 cups.

# mushroom sauce
## sauce duxelles

¼ cup butter
1½ cups chopped mushrooms
¼ cup flour
1¼ cups milk
½ cup white wine
¼ teaspoon salt
3 tablespoons lemon juice
2 egg yolks
1 can shrimp, rinsed and
    drained (optional)

Melt butter. Cook mushrooms until liquid has evaporated. Stir in flour. Add milk and wine. Cook over medium heat, stirring constantly, until thickened. Add salt and lemon juice.
Add small amount of hot sauce to egg yolks, then add egg yolks to sauce, stirring constantly. Heat gently. Stir in shrimp, if desired.
Use sauce with salmon loaf, poached fish, or souffles. Makes 2 cups.

# sauce thickener
## beurre manié

*For 10 tablespoons:*
8 tablespoons butter, softened
8 tablespoons flour

*For 1 tablespoon:*
1 tablespoon butter, softened
1 tablespoon flour

Cream butter and flour. Add 1 tablespoon of mixture to thicken about ¾ cup liquid. Stir in *beurre manié;* bring sauce to boiling point.
This mixture freezes well and is most convenient if placed in an ice-cube tray by tablespoons. Freeze, then transfer to a plastic bag. Add frozen paste directly to sauce.

# meats

## beef in red wine sauce
*boeuf bourguignon*

3 tablespoons vegetable oil
12 small white onions, peeled
2 pounds lean stewing beef, cubed
1 tablespoon flour
2 cups dry red wine
1 cup beef bouillon
1 clove garlic, minced

1 tablespoon tomato paste
¼ teaspoon thyme
1 bay leaf
½ teaspoon parsley
1 teaspoon salt
½ teaspoon pepper
½ pound fresh mushrooms, quartered

Heat oil in large frypan. Saute onions lightly; remove from pan. Add beef cubes; sauté until brown. Sprinkle cubes with flour; toss to coat meat. Cook for 2 minutes, stirring often. Add wine, bouillon, garlic, tomato paste, and seasonings. Stir well, cover, and simmer slowly about 3 hours or until meat is tender. Add more bouillon if necessary. The last hour of cooking, add onions. Add mushrooms the last 15 minutes. If sauce is too thin, reduce it by boiling rapidly or by adding Sauce Thickener (see Index). Adjust seasonings. Serve. Makes 4 to 6 servings.

# filet steaks with herb butter

## filets de boeuf entrecôte bercy

*herb butter*

**4 ounces softened butter**
**1 tablespoon finely chopped parsley**
**1 tablespoon finely chopped chives**
**1 teaspoon dried chervil**
**1 teaspoon dried tarragon**
**1 tablespoon grated shallots or onion**
**Dash of pepper**

**4 filets mignons steaks**
**2 tablespoons vegetable oil**
**½ teaspoon salt**
**⅛ teaspoon pepper**
**4 lemon slices**
**Watercress**
**French-fried potatoes (cut very thin, dried on towels, and deep-fried)**

Make Herb Butter first by blending all ingredients. Spoon onto sheet of waxed paper; shape into a roll about 1½ inches in diameter. Chill butter in freezer while steak is prepared. Cut in 4 thick slices just before serving.

Brush steaks with oil. Depending on thickness, broil about 5 minutes on each side or to desired doneness. Season with salt and pepper.

Arrange steaks on preheated platter. Place 1 lemon slice on each steak; top with slice of Herb Butter. Garnish with watercress and potatoes. Makes 4 servings.

*filet steaks with herb butter*

# veal cutlets with cherry sauce
## côtelettes de veau aux cerises

**4 lean veal cutlets, about 6 ounces each**
**2 tablespoons vegetable oil**
**½ teaspoon salt**
**⅛ teaspoon white pepper**

*cherry sauce*
**¼ cup red wine**
**2 tablespoons evaporated milk**
**½ pound tart canned cherries**
**Parsley for garnish**

Pat cutlets dry with paper towels. Heat oil in frypan. Brown cutlets on each side approximately 3 minutes. Season with salt and pepper. Remove cutlets from pan; keep them warm. Blend wine and evaporated milk in pan; simmer for 3 minutes. Add drained cherries; heat through; adjust seasonings. Return cutlets to sauce; reheat, but do not boil.
Arrange cutlets on preheated platter. Pour Cherry Sauce around them. Garnish with parsley. Makes 4 servings.

*veal cutlets with cherry sauce*

# braised veal rolls
## paupiettes de veau

**6 veal chops or slices**
**1 onion, chopped**
**4 tablespoons vegetable oil**
**4 ounces mushrooms, minced (about 1 cup)**
**1 clove garlic, minced**
**1 cup red wine**
**1 cup chicken broth**

**1 tablespoon tomato paste**
**½ teaspoon salt**
**⅛ teaspoon pepper**
**⅛ teaspoon thyme**
**20 small pitted green olives**
**8 large fresh mushrooms, quartered**
**2 tablespoons Madeira**

Pound veal slices to tenderize and flatten.
In large frypan saute onion in 1 tablespoon hot oil several minutes; add minced mushrooms. Continue cooking for 5 minutes. Spread onion-mushroom mixture on each slice of meat. Roll up; tie with string. Brown veal rolls in 2 tablespoons hot oil. Remove and reserve. Drain excess oil.
Add garlic, wine, broth, tomato paste, salt, pepper, and thyme to frypan. Heat to a simmer; add veal rolls. Cover; simmer for 1½ hours.
Meanwhile, place olives in pan of water; bring to a boil. (This removes some of the salt.) Saute olives and quartered mushrooms in 1 tablespoon hot oil 3 to 4 minutes.
When veal is done, remove it from pan; keep it warm. Strain sauce into clean pan; reduce by boiling, to concentrate flavors and thicken it. Add Madeira, olives, and mushrooms. Heat through. Remove strings from veal rolls. Glaze meat with sauce; garnish with olives and mushrooms. Makes 6 servings.

# veal with artichokes
*noix de veau aux artechauts*

1 clove garlic
1 tablespoon vegetable oil
1 pound veal round, cut into bite-size pieces and pounded
½ teaspoon salt
⅛ teaspoon pepper

1 cup canned tomatoes
¼ cup sherry
¼ teaspoon oregano
1 10-ounce package frozen artichoke hearts

In large frypan sauté garlic in hot oil. Remove garlic; discard. Season veal with salt and pepper. Brown in oil. Add tomatoes, sherry, and oregano; mix well. Add artichoke hearts. Cover; simmer for 1 hour or until meat is tender. Makes 4 servings.


# veal with mushrooms
*sauté de veau aux champignons*

2 pounds boneless, thinly sliced veal cutlet or fillet
½ cup flour
1 teaspoon salt
¼ teaspoon pepper
2 tablespoons vegetable oil

3 tablespoons butter
1 pound sliced mushrooms
6 tablespoons wine
2 tablespoons lemon juice
Lemon slices for garnish

Gently pound veal into very thin pieces.
Mix flour, salt, and pepper. Lightly flour veal.
Melt oil and butter in 10-inch frying pan. Sauté veal until golden brown, about 3 minutes on each side. Remove; keep veal warm.
Add sliced mushrooms to frypan; cook several minutes. Add wine and lemon juice; boil rapidly to reduce sauce slightly.
Pour sauce over veal, garnish with lemon slices, and serve. Makes 6 servings.


# steak diane

3 tablespoons chopped scallions
3 tablespoons vegetable oil
3 tablespoons finely chopped chives
3 tablespoons finely chopped parsley
1 tablespoon Worcestershire sauce

½ teaspoon salt
¼ teaspoon pepper
4 beef steaks, fillets, or rib-eye steaks
¼ cup brandy, warmed

Sauté scallions in 1 tablespoon hot vegetable oil a minute or two. Add chives, parsley, Worcestershire sauce, salt, and pepper.
In second frypan sauté steaks with remaining 2 tablespoons hot vegetable oil until done. (Time depends on thickness of steak.)
Top each steak with some scallion mixture. Flame with warmed brandy until alcohol content is completely burned. Spoon pan juices over steaks. Serve. Makes 4 servings.

# beef braised in red wine
*boeuf à la mode*

3 to 4 pounds boneless beef
roast (rump, sirloin tip, or
round)
½ teaspoon salt
¼ teaspoon freshly ground
black pepper

*marinade*

3 cups red wine
1 cup water
½ cup sliced onions
¼ cup sliced carrots
1 clove garlic, minced
1 bay leaf, crumbled
2 teaspoons chopped fresh
parsley
1 teaspoon thyme

*vegetables*

10 small white onions, peeled
8 carrots, peeled and shaped like small
balls

Parsley for garnish
2 tablespoons flour
2 tablespoons butter
3 tablespoons Madeira
2 tablespoons cognac

*braising ingredients*

2 tablespoons vegetable oil
2 strips lean bacon, cubed
1 ounce brandy, warmed
1 veal or beef knuckle
1 tomato, peeled and
quartered
1 tablespoon chopped fresh
parsley
1 bay leaf
3 green onions, chopped
1 cup beef bouillon
½ teaspoon salt

Rub beef roast with salt; sprinkle with pepper.
Blend all marinade ingredients.
Pour marinade into glass or ceramic bowl. Add beef roast; turn it
several times, so that all sides are coated with marinade. Cover;
marinate in refrigerator 12 to 24 hours. Turn roast occasionally.
Remove roast from marinade; drain; pat dry with paper towels.
Strain and reserve marinade.
Heat oil in large Dutch oven. Add bacon; cook until transparent,
then add roast. Brown well on all sides. Drain off fat. Pour warm
brandy over meat; ignite; wait until flames die down. Add
remaining braising ingredients. Cover pan. Place in preheated
350°F oven. During cooking, occasionally pour some reserved
marinade over roast. Cook roast 3 hours.
Meanwhile, prepare vegetables. Add onions and carrots to Dutch
oven; braise for 1 hour more.
When meat and vegetables are tender, remove meat from oven;
place on preheated platter. Surround with onions and carrots.
Garnish with parsley. Keep food warm.
Strain sauce through fine sieve. Skim off fat, if necessary.
Cream together flour and butter. Thicken pan sauce with all or part
of this. Stir and heat to boiling 1 to 2 minutes. Add Madeira and
cognac. Adjust seasonings. Spoon some sauce over meat; serve the
rest separately. Makes 6 servings.

# beef stroganoff
*sauté de boeuf
á la parisienne*

½ pound fresh mushrooms,
  sliced
2 tablespoons vegetable oil
3 tablespoons butter
2 tablespoons minced green
  onions
½ teaspoon salt
2 pounds beef tenderloin or
  sirloin, cut into ¼-inch-thick
  strips

⅓ cup Madeira
¾ cup beef bouillon
2 teaspoons cornstarch
1 tablespoon cream
1 cup minus 1 tablespoon heavy
  cream
¼ teaspoon pepper
Parsley for garnish

Sauté mushrooms in 1 tablespoon hot oil and 1 tablespoon butter
about 5 minutes or until lightly browned. Add onions; cook for
another minute. Season with ¼ teaspoon salt. Place mushrooms in
a bowl.
Dry meat thoroughly on paper towels.
Place 2 tablespoons butter and 1 tablespoon oil in pan; heat until
butter foam subsides. Saute beef, a few pieces at a time, 1 to 2
minutes on each side. Set sauteed beef aside in separate
bowl.
Pour Madeira and bouillon into frypan; boil it down rapidly while
scraping up browned particles. Reduce liquid to about
⅓ cup.
Blend cornstarch with 1 tablespoon cream. Beat in remaining
cream, then the cornstarch mixture. Simmer for 1 minute. Add
sauteed mushrooms; simmer for 1 minute more. Sauce should be
slightly thickened. Season with ¼ teaspoon salt and pepper. Adjust
seasonings to taste. Add meat to sauce; heat briefly, to just below
simmer, so beef will not overcook.
Garnish stroganoff with parsley. Serve. Makes 4 to 6 servings.

# mediterranean
# beef stew
*boeuf á la catalane*

3 pounds beef chuck, cut into
  1½-inch cubes
¼ cup brandy
½ cup orange juice
4 slices bacon
2 cups sliced onions
3 carrots, peeled and sliced
  ⅛ inch thick
1 1-pound can tomatoes
½ teaspoon salt

⅛ teaspoon pepper
¼ cup chopped parsley
⅛ teaspoon thyme
2 bay leaves
3 cloves garlic, peeled
1 cup red wine
2 small eggplants
1 teaspoon salt
2 tablespoons vegetable oil

Place beef in large covered dish. Pour brandy and orange juice over
meat; marinate for 3 hours.
In Dutch oven sauté bacon to extract some fat. Add onions; sauté
until onions are limp. Add meat, marinade, and remaining
ingredients except eggplants, 1 teaspoon salt, and oil. Bring to
simmer; cover; place in preheated 325°F oven. Bake for
1½ hours.
Meanwhile, remove stem and blossom ends of eggplants. Peel, if
desired; slice, about ½ inch thick. Sprinkle with 1 teaspoon salt.
Toss to coat thoroughly. Let stand 45 minutes. Dry with paper
towels.
Heat oil in frying pan. Cook eggplant until lightly browned. Add to
meat mixture. Bake ½ hour more or until meat is tender. Remove
garlic and bay leaves.
Serve with parslied potatoes. Makes 6 servings.

25

# braised beef with madeira sauce
*boeuf au madère*

*marinade*

1 6-ounce can frozen orange
  juice, thawed
½ cup water
1 tablespoon grated orange peel
2 medium onions, chopped
1 teaspoon salt
½ teaspoon pepper
½ teaspoon ground cloves
1 teaspoon ground coriander
¼ teaspoon ground cumin

3 pounds boneless roast, round
  or chuck
1 tablespoon vegetable oil
1 tablespoon butter
2 tablespoons butter, softened
2 tablespoons flour
2 oranges, sectioned
⅓ cup Madeira
Orange slices for garnish

Place orange juice, water, orange peel, onions, salt, pepper, cloves, coriander, and cumin in blender. Blend until well-mixed (1 to 2 minutes).

Place meat in large bowl. Pour marinade over meat. Marinate in refrigerator 4 to 6 hours. Turn meat once or twice.

Remove meat from marinade; scrape off and reserve marinade.

In Dutch oven sauté beef in oil and 1 tablespoon butter until brown on all sides. Pour reserved marinade over meat; heat to a simmer; cook, covered, for 2½ hours or until meat is tender. Remove meat to preheated platter; keep it warm.

Make *beurre manié* for thickening sauce by creaming butter and flour thoroughly. Blend into juices in Dutch oven, using a wire whisk. Cook over medium heat 5 minutes; stir often. Add orange sections and Madeira; simmer another 5 minutes.

Slice meat; arrange on platter. Spoon sauce over meat. Garnish with orange slices. Serve rest of sauce separately. Makes 6 to 8 servings.

# cold beef in gelatin
*boeuf à la mode en gelée*

Leftover roast beef or Braised
  Beef in Red Wine Sauce (see
  Index)
Basic Aspic (see Index)
Parsley or watercress for garnish

Place meat in bowl slightly larger than meat. Pour Basic Aspic over meat. Cover; refrigerate until gelatin is set. Remove from bowl by placing bowl in sink of cold water to loosen gelatin.

Slice and serve. Garnish platter with parsley or watercress.

# beans with lamb, pork, and sausage
*cassoulet de porc et de mouton*

1 pound Great Northern beans
6 cups water
2 medium onions, chopped
½ teaspoon salt
¼ teaspoon pepper
1 bay leaf
3 whole cloves
2 tablespoons butter
1 tablespoon vegetable oil
1 pound boned lamb (shoulder or leg), cut into 2-inch chunks
½ pound pork, cut into 1½-inch chunks
1 stalk celery, thinly sliced
1 carrot, thinly sliced
2 green onions, chopped
½ pound Polish sausage, thinly sliced
1 cup red wine
2 tablespoons tomato paste
2 cloves garlic, minced
3 tablespoons chopped parsley
Dash cayenne pepper
1 to 2 cups beef bouillon
2 tablespoons packaged bread crumbs

Wash beans. Place beans in pan with 6 cups water. Bring to a boil; boil for 2 minutes; remove from heat; let stand, covered, for 1 hour.
Add onions, salt, pepper, bay leaf, and cloves to beans in their soaking liquid. Cover; cook for 1 hour. When done, drain beans; reserve liquid.
Meanwhile, heat 1 tablespoon butter and oil in frypan; fry lamb and pork until brown. Add celery, carrot, onions, and sausage to meat mixture. Pour in wine; simmer for 40 minutes. Stir in tomato paste, garlic, and parsley. Season with cayenne. Simmer again for 5 minutes, stirring occasionally. Add drained beans; mix thoroughly. Grease ovenproof casserole and spoon in *cassoulet*. Add enough bean liquid or bouillon to come to top of bean-meat mixture. Sprinkle with bread crumbs and dot with 1 tablespoon butter. Bake in preheated 375°F oven 1 hour.
Serve with chunks of French bread and red wine. Makes 6 servings.

*picture on following page: cassoulet*

# beef braised in beer
*carbonnades à la flamande*

½ cup flour
2 teaspoons salt
¼ teaspoon pepper
3 pounds beef chuck or rump, sliced about 2 × 4 × ⅜ inch thick
3 tablespoons peanut oil
4 cups sliced onions
2 cloves garlic, peeled
1 bay leaf
2 tablespoons tomato paste
2 tablespoons brown sugar
½ teaspoon thyme
2 tablespoons chopped parsley
1 cup broth
2 cups beer

Mix flour, salt, and pepper. Dredge beef to coat evenly with flour.
Heat oil in large Dutch oven; brown the meat. Add remaining ingredients; bring to a simmer. Cover tightly. Place in preheated 325°F oven; bake for 2 hours or until meat is tender. Before serving, remove garlic and bay leaf.
Serve beef with boiled potatoes. Makes 6 servings.

27

# stuffed flank steak
## paupiettes de boeuf

2 pounds flank steak, scored, or
  2 round steak, thinly sliced
2 tablespoons Dijon-style
  mustard
¼ teaspoon thyme

*spinach stuffing*

½ package frozen spinach,
  cooked and drained
½ cup chopped onions
1 tablespoon bacon fat or
  vegetable oil
½ cup raw sausage meat

1 egg
½ teaspoon salt
⅛ teaspoon allspice
⅛ teaspoon pepper
1 clove garlic, crushed
¼ cup dry bread crumbs

6 slices bacon
1 onion, chopped
1 carrot, chopped
½ cup dry white wine
1 can beef broth

Spread meat with mustard; sprinkle with thyme.
Squeeze all water from spinach.
Saute ½ cup onions in fat or oil. Add spinach; toss. Add sausage, egg, salt, allspice, pepper, garlic, and crumbs to spinach mixture. Mix well.
Spread stuffing on meat; roll up jelly-roll fashion. Tie with string.
Cook bacon in Dutch oven until partly done. Remove.
Add meat roll to Dutch oven; brown on all sides. This takes about 10 minutes. Lay bacon over meat. Add onion, carrot, wine, and broth. Bring to a simmer. Place in 325°F oven about 1 hour or until tender.
Place meat on platter. Strain juices, pressing hard on vegetables. If desired, thicken with 1 tablespoon cornstarch dissolved in water.
Slice meat; serve with pan juices. Makes 4 to 6 servings.

# stuffed fresh pineapple
## l'ananas farci de jambon

1 fresh pineapple

*ham stuffing*

8 ounces cooked ham, cubed
6 ounces sauerkraut
1 medium apple

*salad dressing*

3 tablespoons mayonnaise
2 tablespoons heavy cream
Juice of 1 lemon
1 teaspoon fresh chopped dill or
  ¼ teaspoon dried dill
¼ teaspoon rosemary
¼ teaspoon sugar
Salt, if desired

Cut pineapple into half lengthwise. Scoop out; cut pineapple into bite-size pieces.
Cube ham.
Rinse and drain sauerkraut.
Core unpeeled apple; cut into thin slices:
Gently mix the above ingredients. Fill the 2 pineapple halves with Ham Stuffing.
Thoroughly blend mayonnaise, cream, lemon juice, dill, rosemary, sugar, and salt.
Pour dressing over salad. Let marinate and chill in refrigerator 30 minutes. Makes 2 servings.

*stuffed fresh pineapple*

# braised leg of lamb mirabeau

*gigot de pré salé*
*braise mirabeau*

4 pounds leg of lamb
½ teaspoon salt
⅛ teaspoon pepper
1 quart buttermilk
¼ cup vegetable oil
2 large carrots, sliced
2 large onions, sliced
2 cups dry white wine
2 cups beef bouillon
1 whole clove garlic

4 tablespoons anchovy paste
(found in gourmet section of
supermarket)
¼ cup heavy cream
1 tablespoon butter
18 flat anchovy fillets, rinsed in
cold water
18 stuffed green olives, cut in half
2 tablespoons fresh chopped
tarragon (or 2 teaspoons dried)

Rinse meat under cold running water; pat dry with paper towels.
Rub with salt and pepper.
Pour buttermilk into large bowl that will hold the lamb. Add lamb;
marinate for 10 hours or overnight.
Drain meat; pat dry with paper towels.
Heat oil in large Dutch oven. Add lamb; brown on all sides about
15 minutes. Remove to a platter.
Brown carrots and onions for 2 to 3 minutes. Remove with slotted
spoon to platter.
Pour out browning oil. Add white wine and reduce it to half by
boiling; scrape up coagulated particles. Place lamb, fattiest-side-up,
in Dutch oven. Surround with vegetables. Pour in enough bouillon
to come two-thirds of the way up the meat. Add garlic; bring liquid
to simmer on top of range. Cover; place in 350°F oven 2½ hours.
Turn and baste meat every half hour. Remove meat; keep it warm.
Strain and degrease cooking liquid. Correct seasoning. Blend
anchovy paste and cream; stir into liquid. Add butter; stir until
melted.
Garnish meat with anchovy fillets and olives; sprinkle with
tarragon. Serve sauce separately. Makes 8 servings.

*braised leg of lamb mirabeau*

# stuffed roast pork
## porc à la châtelaine

6 pounds center-cut loin of pork

*bacon stuffing*

6 strips bacon, diced
2 tablespoons brandy
1 cup chopped prunes
2 cups coarse bread crumbs
   from French bread
1 teaspoon grated lemon rind
3 tablespoons lemon juice
1 cup chicken broth
¼ teaspoon marjoram
½ teaspoon salt
⅛ teaspoon pepper
¼ teaspoon thyme

Cut a pocket in pork roast along ribs.
Fry bacon until crisp; set aside.
Add 2 tablespoons brandy to chopped prunes; let stand 30 minutes.
Mix bread crumbs, lemon rind, lemon juice, broth, and seasonings.
Add bacon and drippings and prunes with liquid.
Use stuffing to fill pocket in pork. Skewer opening closed. Roast in shallow pan at 325°F about 2½ to 3 hours, until 180°F on a meat thermometer.
Serve pork with braised hearts of celery as garnish. Makes 6 servings.

# boiled beef with chicken and vegetables
## pot-au-feu

2 pounds beef chuck or rump
   roast
2 teaspoons salt
2 medium onions, stuck with 3
   cloves each
6 carrots, peeled and cut in half
4 stalks celery (with leaves)
8 cups beef broth
4 sprigs parsley

1 bay leaf
½ teaspoon thyme
2 cloves garlic
8 peppercorns
1 2 to 3-pound chicken, whole
   or selected pieces
½ head cabbage, cut in wedges
4 turnips or potatoes, peeled
   and quartered

In large Dutch oven or roaster (at least 5-quart) place beef, salt, onions, 2 carrots, celery, and broth.
Make a bouquet garni by tying parsley, bay leaf, thyme, garlic, and peppercorns in cheesecloth. Add to stew. Simmer gently 1 hour. If using a whole chicken, add to meat after 1 hour cooking; cook ½ hour more. Add vegetables. If using chicken pieces, cook beef 1½ hours, then add chicken and remaining vegetables. After adding vegetables, cook 30 to 45 minutes longer, until vegetables are done and beef is tender. Remove bouquet garni.
To serve, place broth in soup bowls. Serve as a first course, with rice or noodles if desired. Place meat, chicken, and vegetables on a large platter. Pour over a small amount of broth. Serve. Makes 8 servings.

# poultry

## chicken veronique
*poulet veronique*

⅓ cup flour
½ teaspoon salt
⅛ teaspoon freshly ground
   pepper
1 3- to-4-pound broiler-fryer,
   cut up, or 6 pieces chicken
¼ cup vegetable oil
¼ cup dry white wine

⅓ cup orange juice
4 tablespoons honey
¼ teaspoon salt
1 tablespoon chopped parsley
2 teaspoons grated orange rind
1 cup halved seedless green
   grapes
Orange slices

Mix flour, salt, and pepper. Dredge chicken in flour mixture. Shake
off excess flour. Heat oil in large frying pan or Dutch oven. Brown
chicken pieces on all sides. Drain off oil, if desired. Add wine,
juice, honey, salt, parsley, and orange rind. Cover; simmer over
low heat 45 minutes, until chicken is done. Remove chicken to
serving platter.
Add grapes to pan juices. Heat gently 2 minutes to heat grapes.
Pour sauce over chicken. Garnish with orange slices and additional
green grapes. Makes 4 to 6 servings.

# chicken-filled crepes
*crêpe de volaille*

3 tablespoons butter
¼ cup flour
¼ teaspoon salt
1 cup milk
2 tablespoons sherry
2 tablespoons chopped green
   onion, including tops
1½ cups finely chopped
   cooked chicken
½ cup chopped pecans
8 Basic Crepes (see Index)
½ cup mayonnaise
2 egg whites, stiffly beaten
2 tablespoons grated
   Parmesan cheese

Melt butter in 1-quart saucepan. Stir in flour and salt. Add milk all at once; cook and stir until thickened. Stir in sherry, green onion, chicken and pecans.
Fill each crepe with filling. Roll up; place in greased baking dish.
Fold mayonnaise into egg whites. Spread over tops of crepes.
Sprinkle with cheese. Bake in preheated 375°F oven for 10 minutes.
Makes 4 servings.

# chicken crepe soufflé
*crêpe soufflé de volaille*

*béchamel sauce*

2 tablespoons butter
¼ cup flour
2 cups cold milk
½ teaspoon salt
⅛ teaspoon white pepper

5 cups cooked chicken, chopped
1 pound mushrooms, sliced
   and sautéed
1 lemon, juiced
2 eggs
Dash of cayenne
½ cup heavy cream
8 to 10 Basic Crepes (see Index)

To make sauce, melt butter and blend in flour. Cook for 3 minutes, stirring constantly. Add milk, salt, and pepper; cook until thickened.
Reserve ½ cup sauce. Add chicken, mushrooms, lemon juice, eggs, cayenne, and cream to remaining sauce. Mix well.
Butter a round souffle mold or ovenproof bowl; place crepes on bottom and sides. Fill with chicken mixture; place crepes on top.
Bake in moderate (350°F) oven 30 minutes.
Unmold onto warm platter. Serve with extra Bechamel Sauce.
Makes 6 to 8 servings.

# roast chicken
*poulet rôti*

4 tablespoons butter
½ teaspoon salt
1 3-pound roasting chicken
1 tablespoon dried tarragon
   leaves
1 carrot, cut up

1 onion, peeled and quartered
1 tablespoon vegetable oil
½ tablespoon minced shallots
½ cup chicken broth
2 tablespoons brandy

Spread 1 tablespoon butter and the salt in cavity of chicken. Truss chicken; rub skin with part of remaining butter. Place chicken in shallow roasting pan; surround with tarragon, carrot, and onion. Place in 325°F oven.

Melt remaining butter; add oil. Use this mixture to baste chicken. Baste every 15 to 30 minutes. Chicken will require about 2½ to 3 hours cooking time. Bird is done when juices of inner thigh are clear yellow when pricked with a fork. Remove chicken; allow to stand 15 to 20 minutes before carving.

To make sauce, remove vegetables and all but 2 tablespoons fat. Add shallots; saute until tender. Add broth and brandy; boil rapidly to reduce stock. Serve with chicken. Makes 4 servings.

# poached chicken with vegetables
*poularde bouillie à l'anglaise*

1 small onion
2 cloves garlic, peeled
3 sprigs parsley
1 teaspoon tarragon
1 3-pound chicken
1½ cups dry white wine
1 cup chicken broth
1 teaspoon salt
4 carrots, peeled
4 small turnips, peeled and quartered
4 small leeks, cleaned and
   blanched 5 minutes in boiling
   water (green onions may
   be used)
2 tablespoons flour
½ cup heavy cream
2 egg yolks
2 to 3 teaspoons horseradish

Place onion, garlic, parsley, and tarragon in cavity of chicken; truss. Place chicken in large Dutch oven. Add wine, broth, and salt; bring to a boil. Cover; place in preheated 325°F oven. Bake chicken 45 minutes. Add vegetables. Cover; Bake for 30 minutes longer. When chicken and vegetables are done, remove to serving platter.

Whisk flour into cream.

Skim any fat from pan juices. Beat in cream; heat until thick. Add small amount of gravy to egg yolks, then add egg yolks to pan. Stir and heat through. Add horseradish. Serve sauce with chicken. Makes 4 servings.

# chicken in wine
*coq au vin*

1 3- to-4-pound chicken, cut into serving pieces
⅓ cup vegetable oil
¼ cup cognac
2 medium onions, quartered
1 clove garlic, minced
3 cups Burgundy wine
¼ teaspoon thyme
½ tablespoon tomato paste
1 bay leaf
½ teaspoon salt
⅛ teaspoon pepper

3 strips bacon, cut into 2-inch strips
1 4-ounce can button mushrooms, drained, or ¾ cup small mushrooms, quartered
1 tablespoon butter, softened
1 tablespoon flour
1 or 2 parsley sprigs
2 slices white bread, toasted (optional)

In large Dutch oven brown chicken in hot oil. Drain fat. Pour in cognac; carefully ignite. When flames subside, add onions, garlic, wine, thyme, tomato paste, bay leaf, salt, and pepper. Bring mixture to a boil; simmer, covered, for 1 hour. Skim off fat; correct seasonings. Discard bay leaf.

Meanwhile, place bacon in frypan; cook until done. Remove bacon; sauté mushrooms in hot fat. Drain off fat. Keep bacon and mushrooms warm until needed.

Blend butter and flour together to a smooth paste (*beurre manié*). When chicken is done, add paste to hot liquid. Stir and simmer for a minute or two.

Arrange chicken in casserole or serving dish. Baste with sauce. Garnish with bacon, mushrooms, and parsley. Add toast if desired. Makes 4 servings.

*coq au vin*

# duck with orange sauce
*canard à l'orange*

1 6- to 7-pound duck or 2 3- to 4-pound ducks

½ teaspoon salt
⅛ teaspoon pepper

*orange sauce*

2 tablespoons sugar
2 tablespoons vinegar
Brown Sauce (see Index for recipe, but omit Madeira and cognac)
2 tablespoons frozen orange-juice concentrate

1 teaspoon lemon juice
1 tablespoon cornstarch
1 tablespoon Madeira
2 tablespoons cognac
2 tablespoons Grand Marnier
2 oranges, sectioned

Clean duck; remove giblets. Sprinkle cavity with salt and pepper. Truss; scald with boiling water to open pores so fat will drain out during cooking. Also make small knife slits through skin in thigh, back, and lower breast areas. Roast both sizes of duck at 425°F for 1 hour. Reduce heat to 325°F; cook 6- to 7-pound duck 1 more hour or 3- to 4-pound duck 30 minutes more. If duck is not browned sufficiently, increase heat to 425°F for a few minutes. Meanwhile, make Orange Sauce. Combine sugar and vinegar; boil briefly to caramelize (brown). Cool, add Brown Sauce, and heat to dissolve. Stir in orange and lemon juices; simmer for 8 to 10 minutes. Thicken slightly by mixing cornstarch with Madeira and adding to sauce. Simmer for 1 to 2 1 inutes. Finish sauce with cognac, Grand Marnier, and orange sections.
When duck is roasted, let stand about 10 minutes before carving. Spoon some hot sauce over carved duck; serve rest of sauce separately. Makes 4 servings.

# chicken with chausseur sauce
*poulet sauté chausseur*

½ cup flour
¼ teaspoon salt
Dash pepper
3-pound frying chicken, cut up
2 tablespoons vegetable oil
2 tablespoons butter
2 shallots or green onions
½ pound sliced mushrooms

½ cup white wine
¼ cup brandy
1 cup Basic Brown Sauce (see Index)
1 tablespoon tomato paste
¼ teaspoon thyme
½ teaspoon tarragon
1 tablespoon flour

Mix ½ cup flour, salt, and pepper. Dredge chicken in seasoned flour.
Heat oil and 1 tablespoon butter in Dutch oven or large frypan. Add chicken pieces; cook until lightly browned. Remove chicken. Add shallots and mushrooms to pan. Sauté until liquid from mushrooms has evaporated. Add chicken, wine, brandy, Brown Sauce, and tomato paste. Sprinkle with herbs. Cover; simmer gently until chicken is done, about 30 minutes.
Mix flour and 1 tablespoon butter; add to hot sauce to thicken, if desired.
Serve chicken with sauce separate. Makes 4 servings.

# eggs and cheese

## mushroom quiche
*quiche aux champignons*

3 tablespoons butter
2 tablespoons minced shallots or
    green onions
1 pound sliced fresh mushrooms
1 teaspoon salt
1 teaspoon lemon juice
2 tablespoons Madeira (optional)
3 eggs
1½ cups heavy cream
1 9-inch pie shell, baked 5
    minutes at 425°F
¼ cup grated Swiss cheese

Melt butter in small frying pan. Sauté shallots a few minutes. Add mushrooms, salt, lemon juice, and Madeira. Cook for several minutes, until mushrooms are done and their juice has evaporated. Beat eggs and cream until smooth. Add mushrooms; mix. Pour into pastry shell. Sprinkle cheese on top of quiche. Bake it in preheated 375°F oven 25 to 30 minutes, until a knife inserted in center comes out clean. Serve quiche hot. Makes 6 to 8 servings.

Beat eggs lightly with a fork until well-mixed.

Increase heat under omelet pan to medium-hot, then add butter. Swirl pan around until butter is melted and just beginning to turn brown.

Pour egg mixture into hot pan.

Lightly pull cooked edge away from side of pan, allowing the soft parts to flow underneath.

Tilt pan and slide it back and forth over heat to keep mixture from sticking.

While top is still moist and creamy-looking, fold in half or roll with pancake turner, spatula, or fork.

Hold pan and dish at sharp angle; slide half the omelet onto dish, then flip remaining half over the top.

38

# crepes veronique

The term *veronique* always indicates green grapes

**4 ounces cream cheese**
**1 cup small-curd cottage cheese**
**1 tablespoon sugar**
**Dash salt**
**½ teaspoon grated lemon rind**
**12 Basic Crepes (see Index)**
**½ cup sugar**
**½ cup apple juice or cider**
**¼ cup butter**
**1 tablespoon lemon juice**
**½ teaspoon cinnamon**
**2 cups halved seedless grapes**

Beat cream cheese, cottage cheese, 1 tablespoon sugar, salt, and lemon rind for filling. Fill crepes, using about 2 tablespoons filling for each. Roll crepes; place in greased baking dish. Bake in preheated 350°F oven 15 minutes.
Make sauce in small saucepan by combining ½ cup sugar, apple juice, butter, lemon juice, and cinnamon. Heat until sugar has dissolved. Add grapes; heat through.
Pour sauce over hot crepes. Serve. Makes 6 servings.

# basic omelet and fillings
## omelettes

**2 eggs**
**2 tablespoons water**
**¼ teaspoon salt**
**Dash of pepper**
**1 tablespoon butter**

In small bowl mix eggs, water, salt, and pepper with a fork. Heat butter in 8-inch omelet pan until just hot enough to sizzle a drop of water. Pour in egg mixture. Mixture should start to set immediately. With pancake turner draw cooked portions from edge toward center, so that uncooked portions flow to bottom. Tilt pan as you do this and slide pan back and forth over heat to keep mixture from sticking. Add filling, if desired. While top is still moist and creamy-looking, fold in half or roll with pancake turner. Turn out onto plate with a quick flip of the wrist. Omelets will take about 2 minutes from start to finish. Makes 1 serving.

*omelet fillings*

*cheese*—1 to 2 tablespoons grated Swiss or Parmesan cheese

*herbs*—1 tablespoon minced fresh herbs, such as parsley, chives, or tarragon

*other fillings*—2 to 3 tablespoons sautéed ham or chicken livers, cooked shrimp or crab, cooked asparagus tips, etc.

39

# cheese souffle
*soufflé au fromage*

4 tablespoons butter
3 tablespoons flour
1 cup milk
½ teaspoon salt
Dash pepper
¼ teaspoon dry mustard

1 cup shredded sharp cheddar
  or Swiss cheese
4 eggs, separated
¼ teaspoon cream of tartar
1 tablespoon Parmesan cheese
  or fine bread crumbs

Melt 3 tablespoons butter in 1-quart saucepan. Stir in flour; heat for a few minutes. Add milk all at once. Cook and stir over medium heat until mixture thickens. Stir in salt, pepper, and mustard. Add cheese; cool slightly. Beat in egg yolks.
In medium-size bowl beat egg whites until frothy. Beat in cream of tartar; continue beating egg whites until soft peaks form. Stir ¼ of egg whites into cheese sauce. Gently fold in remaining whites.
Prepare a 1½- or 2-quart soufflé dish by greasing with 1 tablespoon butter and dusting with Parmesan cheese. Pour soufflé into dish; bake in preheated 375°F oven 25 to 30 minutes. Soufflé is done when it is puffed and golden and looks slightly dry, not shiny.
Serve soufflé at once, with a sauce if desired. Makes 4 servings.

# spinach soufflé
*soufflé aux épinards*

5 tablespoons butter
1 tablespoon minced shallots or
  green onions
¾ cup chopped frozen spinach,
  thawed
Dash nutmeg
3 tablespoons flour

1 cup milk
½ teaspoon salt
Dash pepper
4 eggs, separated
¼ teaspoon cream of tartar
1 tablespoon Parmesan cheese
  or bread crumbs

Melt 1 tablespoon butter in small pan. Sauté shallots several minutes, until tender. Add spinach; cook a few minutes to remove moisture. Add nutmeg; set aside.
Melt remaining 3 tablespoons butter in 1-quart saucepan. Stir in flour; cook for several minutes. Add milk all at once. Add salt and pepper. Cook and stir over medium heat until sauce thickens. Stir in spinach. Cool sauce slightly, then add egg yolks. Mix well.
In medium-size bowl beat egg whites until frothy. Beat in cream of tartar; continue beating until soft peaks form. Stir ¼ of egg whites into spinach mixture. Gently fold in remaining whites.
Prepare 1½- or 2-quart soufflé dish by greasing with 1 tablespoon butter and dusting with Parmesan cheese. Pour soufflé into prepared dish. Bake in preheated 375°F oven 25 to 30 minutes. Soufflé is done when golden, puffed, and somewhat dry, not shiny.
Serve soufflé at once, with a sauce if desired. Makes 4 servings.

*Note:* To form a "high-hat" soufflé, use a knife perpendicular to edge of dish. Draw a circle through soufflé 1 inch from the edge and about 1 inch deep.

# seafood

## sole with mushrooms
*sole bonne femme*

1 cup fresh mushrooms
2 tablespoons minced shallots
2 tablespoons chopped parsley
½ teaspoon salt
Dash pepper
1½ pounds sole fillets
½ cup dry white wine (more, if needed)
2 tablespoons flour
2 tablespoons butter
2 to 4 tablespoons heavy cream

Mix mushrooms, shallots, parsley, salt, and pepper. Place in greased flat baking dish. Place fish over mushrooms. Add enough wine to cover bottom of dish. Bring to a simmer. Cover with foil. Place in preheated 350°F oven 15 to 20 minutes, until fish is opaque. Remove fish; keep it warm.

Mix flour and butter.

Boil the juices remaining from fish until they are reduced by one-half. Beat in flour-butter mixture; cook until thickened. Add juices that have drained from fish and enough cream to make a medium sauce.

Pour sauce over fish. Serve. Makes 4 servings.

# fried trout grenoble
*truites grenobloise*

4 freshwater trout, fresh or
    frozen (each about ½ pound)
Juice of 1 lemon
Salt
5 tablespoons flour
½ cup vegetable oil
¼ cup butter
1 slice dry bread, crumbled
2 tablespoons capers
1 lemon, sliced
Parsley sprigs for garnish

Thoroughly wash fish; pat dry with paper towels. Sprinkle with half the lemon juice; let stand 5 minutes. Salt trout inside and out; roll it in flour.
Heat oil in frypan. Add trout; fry for 5 minutes on each side or until golden. Remove fish carefully with slotted spoon; discard oil. Melt butter in same frypan. Return trout to pan; fry for 5 minutes on each side. Remove; arrange on preheated platter.
Add bread crumbs to butter; cook until browned. Pour over trout. Sprinkle rest of lemon juice over trout. Top with drained capers. Garnish with lemon slices and parsley sprigs. Makes 4 servings.

# poached fish
*filets de poisson pochés au vin blanc*

5 cups boiling water
2 medium onions, sliced
1 carrot, chopped
1 stalk celery
4 sprigs parsley
1 bay leaf
2 tablespoons salt
1 lemon, sliced

2 cups dry white wine
8 fish fillets or 1 3- to-4-pound
    whole dressed fish
2 tablespoons butter
2 tablespoons flour
½ cup heavy cream
1 egg yolk
1 tablespoon lemon juice

In 3-quart saucepan combine water, onions, carrot, celery, parsley, bay leaf, salt, and lemon. Bring to a boil. Reduce heat; simmer for 15 minutes. Add wine; simmer 15 minutes longer. Strain liquid. Cool to lukewarm.
Place fresh fillets in bottom of greased casserole. Cover with above stock. Bring just to simmer on the range. Cover tightly; place in preheated 325°F oven. Cook fish 10 to 15 minutes, until done, or simmer on top of stove. If poaching a whole fish, first wrap in cheesecloth. Then place fish in large shallow pan, such as a French fish-poacher; cover with liquid. Cook fish at simmer about 10 minutes per inch of thickness. Remove from heat; leave fish in broth while preparing sauce.
To prepare sauce for fish, melt butter in small pan. Add flour; stir to blend. Add 1 cup of the poaching liquid. Cook, stirring constantly, until thickened.
Mix cream and egg yolk. Stirring rapidly, add cream and lemon juice to sauce. Keep sauce warm. Serve over fish. Makes 8 servings.

*picture on opposite page: fried trout grenoble*

*bouillabaisse*

# seafood stew
*bouillabaisse*

2 tablespoons vegetable oil
2 onions, chopped, or
   3 leeks, sliced
4 cloves garlic, crushed
2 fresh tomatoes, peeled
   and diced
3 tablespoons tomato paste
2 cups bottled clam juice
4 cups chicken bouillon
1 tablespoon salt
⅛ teaspoon pepper
¼ teaspoon saffron
½ teaspoon thyme
1 bay leaf
6 sprigs parsley
Grated rind of 1 orange

*seafoods*
1 2-pound lobster and/or other
   shellfish, such as clams,
   mussels (with shells), scallops,
   crab, or shrimp
2 pounds assorted white fish
   fillets, such as sea bass,
   perch, cod, sole, flounder, or
   red snapper
Chopped parsley for garnish

Heat vegetable oil in large saucepan or Dutch oven. Saute onions or leeks several minutes, until translucent. Add remaining sauce ingredients; simmer 45 minutes.

Prepare seafoods by cooking lobster. (Place in large kettle of boiling salted water 10 minutes.) Break claws and tail from body; crack claws; cut tail into 1-inch chunks. Remove black vein from tail pieces; leave shell on meat. Wash and cut fish fillets into 2-inch pieces.

Add lobster and firm-fleshed fish (sea bass, perch, etc.) to boiling sauce. Boil rapidly 5 minutes, then add tender-fleshed fish, such as clams, scallops, sole, or cod. Boil another 5 minutes. Lift seafoods out as soon as cooked; keep them warm in soup tureen or platter. Boil liquid 10 minutes to reduce. Strain liquid through coarse sieve into tureen, mashing through some of the vegetables. Garnish with parsley. Serve. Makes 6 servings.

# sole with tomatoes
*sole duglére*

1 pound tomatoes, peeled,
   seeded, and chopped (about
   1½ cups)
2 tablespoons minced shallots
2 tablespoons minced parsley
½ teaspoon salt
Dash pepper
1½ pounds sole fillets

¾ cup dry white wine
¼ cup water or clam juice
2 tablespoons butter or
   margarine
2 tablespoons flour
½ teaspoon sugar
3 to 4 tablespoons heavy cream

Mix tomatoes, shallots, parsley, salt, and pepper; place in bottom of greased flat baking dish. Place fillets over tomatoes. Add wine and water; bring to simmer on the range. Cover with aluminum foil. Place in preheated 325°F oven 13 to 15 minutes, until fish is opaque. Remove fish to serving dish; keep it warm.
Boil juices until mixture is reduced to about one-half.
Mix butter and flour. Stir into juices; cook until thickened. Add sugar, cream, and juices drained from fish on platter.
Pour sauce over fish. Serve. Makes 4 servings.

# scallops
*coquilles au naturel*

1 pound scallops
2 tablespoons chopped shallots,
   or green onions
6 tablespoons butter

1 teaspoon lemon juice
⅓ cup fine bread crumbs
2 tablespoons chopped parsley

Wash scallops to remove sand; dry on paper towels. Place scallops in 4 buttered shells or in a buttered casserole.
Sauté shallots in 2 tablespoons butter until soft. Distribute evenly over scallops.
Melt remaining butter. Add lemon juice. Pour over scallops; sprinkle with crumbs. Bake in preheated 375°F oven 12 to 15 minutes, until scallops are tender when pierced with a knife.
Serve scallops very hot, garnished with chopped parsley. Makes 4 servings.

# baked salmon loaf
*pain de saumon
(coulibiac)*

2 tablespoons butter
¼ cup finely chopped celery
2 tablespoons chopped shallots
   or green onions
½ cup chopped mushrooms
2 cups cooked or canned salmon
   (2 1-pound cans)
1½ cups soft bread crumbs

½ teaspoon dried chervil
2 tablespoons lemon juice
3 eggs, beaten
2 tablespoons chopped parsley
1 cup evaporated milk or
   heavy cream
2 tablespoons brandy
Mushroom Sauce (see Index)

Melt butter in small frying pan. Cook celery and shallots several minutes. Add mushrooms; cook until liquid has evaporated. Place mushroom mixture in 2-quart bowl with remaining ingredients; mix thoroughly. Pour into well-greased 9 × 5 × 3-inch loaf pan or 2-quart fish mold. Bake salmon in preheated 350°F oven 40 to 45 minutes, until done in the center.
Unmold salmon. Serve with Mushroom Sauce. Makes 6 servings.

# salmon mousse
*mousse de saumon*

The mousse is best served as an hors d'oeuvre, since it is very rich.

2 tablespoons gelatin
1½ cups fish stock, from
  poaching fish (or 1½ cups
  bottled clam juice)
½ cup mayonnaise
1 tablespoon lemon juice
1 1-pound salmon steak,
  cooked, boned, and mashed,
  or 2 cups canned salmon

1 tablespoon Madeira
¼ teaspoon salt
⅛ teaspoon white pepper
½ cup heavy cream, whipped
Lemon or cucumber slices for
  garnish

Sprinkle gelatin over ½ cup cold stock, then heat stock to dissolve gelatin completely. With wire whisk, beat in mayonnaise and lemon juice. Cool until slightly thickened. Fold in salmon and Madeira. Add salt and pepper to taste. Gently fold in whipped cream. Pour into oiled 2-quart fish mold. Chill until set.
Unmold mousse to serve. Garnish with lemon or cucumber slices. Makes a 2-quart mold, 8 to 12 servings.

# stuffed fillets of sole
*filets de sole farcis*

*shrimp stuffing*

2 tablespoons minced shallots
  or green onions
2 tablespoons butter or
  margarine
½ pound mushrooms, sliced
2 tablespoons chopped parsley
½ pound tiny shrimp, cooked
  and cleaned

6 fillets of sole
2 tablespoons butter
2 tablespoons flour
1 cup dry white wine
½ cup heavy cream or
  half-and-half
¼ teaspoon salt
2 tablespoons brandy
½ cup grated Swiss cheese

Cook shallots in 2 tablespoons melted butter until transparent. Add mushrooms; cook until all liquid has evaporated. Add parsley and shrimp.
Place about 2 tablespoons stuffing on large end of each fillet. Roll up fillets; place in greased flat baking dish (12 × 8 × 2 inches). Melt 2 tablespoons butter; mix with flour. Add white wine; cook until thick. Stir in cream, salt, and brandy. Add any remaining stuffing to sauce. Pour sauce over fillets. Bake in preheated 400°F oven about 20 to 25 minutes, until fish is done. Sprinkle with Swiss cheese the last 5 minutes of baking. The top should be golden brown. Makes 6 servings.

# salmon steaks with hollandaise sauce
*filets de saumon hollandaise*

¼ pound fresh small
  mushrooms
1 tablespoon butter
½ cup white wine
6 tablespoons water
½ teaspoon salt
⅛ teaspoon white pepper
4 salmon steaks, each about 6
  to 8 ounces

Juice of ½ lemon
1 recipe Hollandaise Sauce (see
  Index)
8 ounces fresh oysters
1 4½-ounce can deveined
  shrimp
1 ounce truffles, sliced
  (optional, found in
  specialty stores)

Clean mushrooms; cut into thin slices.
Heat butter in frypan. Add mushrooms; sauté for 3 minutes. Add ¼ cup wine and the water. Season with salt and pepper; simmer for 10 minutes.
Meanwhile, rinse salmon steaks under cold running water; pat dry. Sprinkle with lemon juice. Let stand 5 minutes.
Strain mushrooms, reserving juice. Set mushrooms aside.
Add mushroom juice to frypan. Add rest of wine. Bring to a boil; add salmon steaks. Cover; simmer over low heat 20 minutes.
While salmon is cooking, prepare Hollandaise Sauce. Keep it warm.
Remove salmon steaks with slotted spoon to preheated platter. Keep them warm.
Add oysters to simmering stock. Heat about 5 minutes or until edges begin to curl. Add shrimp; just heat through. Remove; drain. Spoon around salmon steaks.
Pour Hollandaise Sauce over salmon. Garnish with reserved reheated mushrooms and truffle slices if desired. Makes 4 servings.
.

# scallops with mushrooms
*coquilles st. jacques à la parisienne*

1½ pounds scallops
½ cup butter
1 cup dry white wine
½ teaspoon salt
⅛ teaspoon pepper
1 green onion, minced
4 tablespoons flour
1 cup heavy cream
1 cup milk

½ pound fresh mushrooms,
  sliced
Drops of lemon juice
Salt and pepper to taste
1 tablespoon cognac
2 tablespoons butter
6 scallop shells or pyrex dishes
Roe for garnish (optional)

Wash scallops well in slightly salted water to remove all grit. Drain and dry on paper towels. Cut scallops in half or in fourths to make them bite-size.
In medium saucepan bring ½ cup butter, wine, ½ teaspoon salt, 1/8 teaspoon pepper, and onion to simmer. Add scallops; return to simmer. Cover; simmer slowly 5 minutes. Remove scallops with slotted spoon; set aside.
Boil pan liquids; reduce to just the butter. Add flour; cook, stirring for 3 minutes. Stir in cream, milk, mushrooms, lemon juice, and salt and pepper to taste. Over medium heat, cook until thickened, stirring frequently. Add cognac. Blend two-thirds of sauce with scallops.
Grease shells or dishes. Divide scallop mixture between them. Cover with rest of sauce. Dot with 2 tablespoons butter.
Just before serving, place in preheated 400°F oven; heat about 10 minutes or until sauce is bubbling. Garnish with roe, if available. Makes 6 servings.

# breads

## crusty rolls
*brioche*

1 package dry yeast
¼ cup warm water
½ cup butter
¼ cup sugar
1 teaspoon salt
3¼ cups all-purpose flour

½ cup milk
¾ cup cake flour
4 eggs
Water
1 egg yolk
1 tablespoon water

Soften yeast in ¼ cup warm water (110°F). Cream butter, sugar, and salt with electric beater. Beat 1 cup all-purpose flour and the milk into creamed mixture. Add cake flour, eggs, and softened yeast; beat well. Beat in remaining flour. Beat by hand 6 to 10 minutes. Cover; let rise in warm place until double in bulk (about 2 hours).

Stir down dough. Beat well. Turn out dough onto floured board. Form a long roll. Cut off ¼ of dough; set aside. Cut remaining dough into 6 pieces; form each piece into 4 balls. Tuck under cut edges; place in greased individual brioche pans or greased muffin pans. Cut reserved dough into 6 pieces; cut each of 6 pieces into 4 pieces. Shape 24 balls. Make small indentations in middles of large balls; brush holes with water. Press small balls into indentations. Beat egg yolk and 1 tablespoon water. Brush tops of balls. Cover; let rise until double (about 30 minutes). Bake at 375°F about 15 minutes or until golden. Brush again with yolk mixture. Bake for 5 more minutes. Remove from pans immediately. Brioches may be frozen and reheated in a 350°F oven. Makes 24 rolls.

# french bread
*pain ordinaire*

7 cups all-purpose flour
1 cup cake flour
2 packages active dry yeast
2½ cups water
1 tablespoon sugar
1 tablespoon salt
1 tablespoon butter
1 to 2 tablespoons cornmeal
1 egg white
1 tablespoon water

In large bowl combine 2½ cups all-purpose flour, cake flour, and yeast.

Heat 2½ cups water, sugar, salt, and butter until just warm (115 to 120°F). Butter may not be completely melted. Add to flour-yeast mixture; beat for 3 minutes with an electric mixer, scraping bowl often. By hand, stir in enough remaining flour to make a soft dough. Place dough on floured surface; let rest for 10 minutes.

Knead dough until smooth and elastic (about 12 to 15 minutes). Add small amounts of flour to kneading surface to prevent sticking, but do not add too much; dough must remain soft. After kneading, shape dough into a ball. Place in greased bowl; turn greased-side-up. Cover; let rise until double (1 to 1½ hours).

Punch down dough. Divide in half for 2 loaves or fourths for 4 loaves. Roll each piece into a rectangle about ½ inch thick. Roll up tightly from the long side; pinch to seal edges and ends.

Grease 2 baking sheets; coat with cornmeal. Place loaves diagonally on baking sheets. Cut ¼-inch diagonal gashes across tops every 2 inches.

Beat egg white with a fork; add 1 tablespoon water. Brush tops and sides of loaves with egg white. Cover; let rise until double (about 1 hour).

Preheat oven to 400°F. Place flat pan of boiling water on lowest rack of oven. Bake bread until light brown, about 20 minutes. Brush again with glaze. Lower heat to 375°F. Bake for 10 to 20 minutes, depending on size of loaves. Remove from baking sheets; cool. Makes 2 large or 4 small loaves.

# basic crepes
*pâté à crêpes*

3 eggs
⅛ teaspoon salt
1½ cups flour
1½ cups milk
2 tablespoons vegetable oil or
  melted butter
1 teaspoon sugar (Dessert
  Crepes only)

*Blender method:* Combine ingredients in blender jar; blend about 1 minute. Scrape down sides with rubber spatula; blend for another 15 seconds or until smooth.

*Mixer or whisk method:* In medium mixing bowl, combine eggs and salt. Gradually add flour, alternating with milk. Beat until smooth. Beat in oil or melted butter and sugar if desired. Makes approximately 24 crepes.

*technique for making crepes*

You can use your pan to make crepes either upside down or right side up. To use it upside down, preheat pan and dip bottom into batter in a 9-inch pie pan. Hold hot pan bottom in batter only a moment. Gently lift pan up; turn it over. Immediately return upside-down pan to heat, so that the flame or hot element is beneath inside of pan. Cook until batter loses its wet look and—with most batters—a very slight browning begins to show on edge of crepe. Remove from heat. Turn pan over; gently loosen outer edge of crepe with a thin plastic, wooden, or Teflon® -coated pancake turner or spatula. The crepe should fall onto the stack already cooked. If not, loosen center of crepe with a spatula.
To use pan right side up, put about 1 tablespoon oil in pan; heat until oil is hot. Tip out oil. A little will cling to pan surface; this will be enough to cook the crepes. A well-seasoned pan needs no additional oil. Return pan to medium-high heat. With one hand pour in 2 to 3 tablespoons batter. At same time lift pan above heat source with your other hand. Immediately tilt pan in all directions, swirling batter so it covers bottom of pan in a very thin layer.
Work quickly, before batter cooks too much to swirl. Return to heating unit; cook over medium-high heat. Cook crepe until bottom is browned. Slide knife or spatula under edge of crepe to loosen it. Then carefully turn with a spatula. Brown other side a few seconds. Remove from heat; shake pan to loosen crepe; slide crepe from pan with spatula or knife. Add to stack of already cooked crepes.
The batter should be about the consistency of light cream. If it gets too thick while it is standing, thin batter by adding more liquid. If batter becomes too thin, put it into a blender and add more flour.
If batter forms a clump in the middle of pan, pan is too hot. Wave pan about in the air to cool it down; lower heat.
Crepes have an inside and an outside. The side that cooks first is the outside because it looks more attractive. The inside of crepe is rolled or folded into direct contact with the filling.

*Place oiled crepe or omelet pan over medium-low heat; heat until oil is hot. Tip out oil. Oil that clings to pan will be enough to cook crepes. Or, brush heated pan with oil.*

*Return pan to medium-high heat. Then lift pan from heat and pour the batter on the side in a very thin layer.*

*Immediately swirl pan so batter completely covers the bottom in a very thin layer. Return to heat. Cook crepe until it is browned.*

*Slide a knife or spatula under edge of crepe to loosen.*

*Lift carefully with a spatula and turn over gently. Brown other side for several seconds.*

*Remove from heat. Shake pan to loosen crepe; slide crepe from pan. Continue cooking crepes until all batter is used.*

# crescent rolls
## *croissants*

1½ cups butter
¼ cup all-purpose flour
2 packages dry yeast
½ cup warm water
¾ cup milk
3 tablespoons sugar

1 teaspoon salt
1 egg
3½ to 4¼ cups all-purpose
　flour
1 egg yolk
1 tablespoon milk

Soften butter to room temperature. Cream butter with ¼ cup all-purpose flour. Roll mixture between waxed paper to a 12 × 6-inch rectangle. Chill at least 1 hour.

Soften yeast in warm water (110°F).

Heat ¾ cup milk, sugar, and salt in small pan. Stir to dissolve sugar. Cool to lukewarm. Beat in softened yeast and 1 egg. Beat in 2 cups flour. Add enough remaining flour to make a soft but not sticky dough.

Knead dough on floured board until smooth and elastic (10 to 20 minutes). Roll out to a 15-inch square. Place chilled butter on one half; fold over other half; seal edges. Roll to a 21 × 12-inch rectangle; seal edges. Fold in thirds. It may be necessary to chill dough between rollings if butter becomes soft. Repeat rolling and folding dough 2 more times. Seal edges; chill dough 45 minutes.

Cut dough crosswise in fourths. Cut out a cardboard triangle with a 4-inch base and 4½-inch sides. Roll out each piece in a long strip about 6 inches wide and ¼ inch thick. Lay cardboard triangle on dough; cut out a triangle with sharp knife. Reverse cardboard triangle on dough every other time. Roll loosely from base of triangle toward point, stretching slightly to make dough thinner. Place on ungreased baking sheets, point down, with ends curled. Press ends to cookie sheet. Roll small pieces also. Cover; let rise at 85°F until double (about 1½ hours).

Beat egg yolk with 1 tablespoon milk; *gently* brush on rolls. Bake in preheated 375°F oven about 15 minutes. Remove from sheets to cool.

Serve part of this recipe as Dessert Croissants (see Index). Freeze cooled croissants in plastic bags. Reheat on baking sheet at 375°F about 10 minutes. Makes about 24 rolls.

# desserts

## floating island
*oeufs à la neige*

**3 eggs, separated**
**Dash salt**
**¾ cup sugar**
**2 cups milk**
**1 tablespoon cornstarch**
**1 teaspoon vanilla**

Beat egg whites with salt in small (1½-quart) bowl until foamy. Gradually add ½ cup sugar, 1 tablespoon at a time, Continue beating until sugar is dissolved and whites form very stiff peaks. Pour milk into large frying pan; heat to very warm.
Make snowballs (or egg shapes) from meringue, using 2 spoons. Drop each snowball into hot milk. Poach for 2 minutes on one side, turn gently, and poach for 2 minutes more. It's important that milk not boil, or an off-flavor will develop. When snowballs are done, remove from milk; drain on paper towels.
Beat egg yolks until lemon-colored. Beat in remaining ¼ cup sugar and cornstarch. Beat until well-blended. Add hot milk to egg yolks, beating constantly. Pour mixture into 1-quart saucepan; cook over medium heat until custard thickens. Add vanilla; strain, if desired. Cool.
Spoon custard into large serving dish or individual dishes. Float snowballs on top. Serve chilled. Makes 4 servings.

## pears in chocolate sauce
### poires au chocolat

**1 large can pear halves (29-ounce)**

*chocolate sauce*

**8 ounces semisweet chocolate**
**2 tablespoons hot water**
**1 tablespoon butter**
**1 egg yolk**
**½ cup heavy cream**
**1 egg white**

*pears in chocolate sauce*

Drain pear halves; arrange in 6 individual serving dishes.
Place chocolate in top of double boiler. Stir in hot water; melt chocolate over boiling water. Remove from heat. Stir in butter until melted. Add egg yolk and heavy cream.
Beat egg white until stiff peaks form; fold into Chocolate Sauce.
Spoon Chocolate Sauce over pears. Serve immediately. Makes 6 servings.

## pastry cream
### crème pâtissière

**⅔ cup sugar**
**3 egg yolks**
**⅓ cup flour**
**1½ cups boiling milk**
**1 tablespoon butter**

**⅓ cup ground almonds (optional)**
**¼ teaspoon almond extract (optional)**
**1 teaspoon vanilla**

In small bowl beat sugar and egg yolks until mixture forms a ribbon on the surface, which slowly dissolves when beaters are lifted. Gradually beat in flour; beat until smooth. Slowly add hot milk, beating constantly. Pour mixture into 1-quart saucepan; cook over low heat until mixture thickens, stirring constantly. Add butter, almonds, and extracts.
Cool Pastry Cream. Use for tarts or other desserts. Keeps several days, but must be refrigerated. Makes 2 cups.

# basic pastry dough
*pâté brisée*

| 2 cups flour | ½ cup vegetable oil |
| 1 teaspoon salt | 5 tablespoons cold water |

Sift together flour and salt.
Pour oil and cold water into measuring cup (do not stir). Add liquid to flour mixture; stir gently with a fork. Form into 2 balls. Roll each flattened ball between 2 sheets of waxed paper until correct size for pan. Peel off top sheet of waxed paper; invert dough into pie plate. Remove paper. Fit into pan, trim crust to ½ inch beyond edge, fold under, and flute edge. Bake at 350°F for 10 to 12 minutes or until golden brown. Makes 2 layers for 8-inch pan. (Divide recipe in half for 1 layer.)

# sweet pastry dough
*pâté brisée sucrée*

| 2 cups flour | ¾ cup unsalted butter |
| 2 tablespoons sugar | 1 egg yolk |
| ¼ teaspoon salt | 4 tablespoons cold water |

Mix flour, sugar, and salt. Cut in butter until coarse crumbs form. Add egg yolk and water; gently mix to form a dough. Wrap in waxed paper; chill dough 1 hour. Divide dough in half. Save half for later use.
To bake, roll dough; press into pie or tart pan. Prick with fork. Bake in preheated 425°F oven 10 to 15 minutes, until golden brown. Makes crust for 2 9-inch shells.

# puff pastry
*pâté feuillettée*

| 4 sticks (1 pound) unsweetened butter | 1 teaspoon salt |
| 4 cups all-purpose flour | 1 tablespoon lemon juice |
| 2 tablespoons cornstarch | 1¼ cups cold water |

Cut each stick of butter into 3 lengthwise strips. Place all 12 strips on waxed paper, side by side, to form a rectangle. With rolling pin, shape into 6 × 12-inch rectangle. Refrigerate butter until ready to use.
Mix flour, cornstarch, and salt in mixing bowl.
Add lemon juice to water. Add liquid to flour. Knead gently several minutes to form a dough. Wrap dough in plastic wrap and refrigerate. Let rest ½ hour.
Pat or roll dough, on lightly floured board, into 18 × 6-inch rectangle. Place chilled butter over upper ⅔ of dough, spreading it to within ½ inch of edges. Dough will be rough-looking. The lower third is unbuttered. Fold bottom ⅓ up to middle; fold top ⅓ down to cover it. Turn dough so top flap is at the right. Roll dough to a 16 × 6-inch rectangle. Fold top and bottom to the middle, then fold all dough in half. This completes the second turn. The dough will look smooth.
Traditionally, the dough is marked with 2 depressions made with the fingertips. Refrigerate dough 30 to 60 minutes.
Repeat above procedure, making 2 or more turns. Mark dough with 4 fingers. You may use dough now or repeat, making 6 or 8 turns. However, before shaping, chill dough 2 hours.
The dough may be used for Napoleons, Cream Horns, or patty shells. It can also be used for appetizers. The dough can be stored in refrigerator for several days, or frozen up to 1 year. Makes 2½ pounds dough.

**Note:** After chilling dough, it may be necessary to beat dough with rolling pin to soften the butter and aid rolling.

55

# molded ice cream
*bombe glasée*

1 quart coffee ice cream, softened
¾ cup chopped nuts
1 quart chocolate ice cream, softened
1 pint vanilla ice cream, softened
2 tablespoons brandy
2 ounces unsweetened chocolate, melted and cooled
¼ cup light corn syrup
1 egg

Line 2-quart bowl or mold with heavy-duty aluminum foil.
Blend coffee ice cream with ½ cup nuts. Line mold with coffee ice cream. Freeze until firm (about 1 hour).
Use softened chocolate ice cream to form second layer, leaving a deep hole in center. Freeze until firm.
Blend vanilla ice cream and brandy. Fill hole; smooth bottom of mold. Freeze several hours.
Turn out ice cream onto cold tray. Carefully remove foil; return to freezer.
Combine chocolate, corn syrup, and egg; beat 4 minutes.
Working quickly, spread frosting over molded ice cream. Garnish with remaining ¼ cup nuts. Slice to serve. Makes 8 servings.

# baked caramel custard
*crème renversée au caramel*

1 cup sugar
¼ cup water
1 4- to 6-cup metal mold
4 eggs
2 egg yolks
2½ cups milk, hot
Dash of salt
1 teaspoon vanilla

Put ½ cup sugar and ¼ cup water into mold. Heat until sugar caramelizes and turns dark brown. Immediately dip mold into pan of cold water for 2 to 3 second to cool. Tilt pan so that mixture films bottom and sides of mold with caramel.
Combine eggs, yolks, and ½ cup sugar in medium-size bowl. Beat until well-mixed and foamy. Stir in 1¼ cups hot milk; mix well. Add remaining milk, salt, and vanilla; stir well. Strain sauce through sieve to remove any coagulated egg. Pour into mold. Skim off foam on top. Preheat oven to 325°F.
Set mold in larger pan. Pour boiling water around mold to come halfway up its sides. Place on lowest rack of oven. Bake custard 45 minutes or until center is firm. Cool, then refrigerate custard.
When ready to unmold, run a knife around edge; set in lukewarm water 1 to 2 minutes. Place serving plate upside down over mold; quickly invert. Makes 4 servings.

# pear tart with almond cream
*tarte aux poires*

½ recipe Sweet Pastry Dough (see Index)
½ recipe Pastry Cream (see Index)
½ cup sugar
1 cup water
4 ripe pears, peeled and sliced
¼ cup apricot preserves

Roll pastry 1/8 inch thick; fit into tart shell with removable bottom or into 9-inch pie pan. Bake in preheated 425°F oven 5 minutes. Cool. When cool, spread with Pastry Cream.
Dissolve sugar and water in 1 quart saucepan. Gently poach pears 3 to 4 minutes, until tender. Remove pears from syrup. Arrange in rows over Pastry Cream.
Heat preserves; press through sieve. Spread glaze thinly over pears. Bake tart 5 to 8 minutes more at 425°F. Serve at room temperature or chilled. Makes 8 servings.

# strawberry tarts
*tartelettes aux fraises*

1 recipe Sweet Pastry Dough
(see Index)
6 egg yolks
½ cup sugar
½ cup flour
2 cups whole milk

2 tablespoons butter
1 tablespoon vanilla
1 cup apricot jam or jelly
2 tablespoons sugar
1 pint strawberries

Make pastry; place on or in tart molds; bake.
To make cream, place yolks in heavy-bottomed saucepan; beat in
½ cup sugar with wire whip. Continue beating about 2 minutes.
Beat in flour, then hot milk in a thin stream. Place pan over
moderate heat; stir slowly and continuously with whip until mixture
thickens. As it becomes lumpy, beat vigorously to smooth it out.
Lower heat; continue cooking for several minutes to thicken the
cream. Prevent scorching cream in bottom of pan by stirring and
not using high heat. Remove from heat; beat in butter and vanilla.
Cover; chill.
Prepare glaze by boiling jam or jelly with 2 tablespoons sugar
several minutes, until drops falling from spoon are thick and sticky
(228°F). Place pan in hot water until ready to use.
Spread a layer of cream about ½ inch deep in shells. Arrange
fresh, hulled strawberries, stem-ends-down, in shell over cream.
Spoon warm glaze over strawberries. Chill until ready to serve. Best
if served within an hour. Makes 8 to 10, depending on size of tart
molds.

# dessert croissants
*croissants a la gelée
de groseilles*

4 tablespoons apricot jam or
red currant jelly
3 tablespoons water
6 hot Croissants (see Index),
freshly made or reheated

1 tablespoon corn syrup
1 teaspoon cognac
1 teaspoon lemon juice
About ¼ cup powdered sugar

Boil jam or jelly with 2 tablespoons water 1 minute. With pastry
brush, coat hot Croissants with mixture.
Boil corn syrup and 1 tablespoon water 1 minute. Off heat, add
cognac and lemon juice. Stir in enough powdered sugar to make a
thin paste. Spread over jam coating.
Serve Croissants while warm. Makes 6 servings.

# chocolate mousse
*mousseline au chocolat*

8 ounces semisweet chocolate
pieces
2 tablespoons water
¼ cup powdered sugar
½ cup unsalted butter, softened

6 eggs, separated
1 tablespoon dark rum
½ teaspoon vanilla
2 tablespoons sugar

Melt chocolate and 2 tablespoons water in double boiler. When
melted, stir in powdered sugar; add butter bit by bit. Set aside.
Beat egg yolks until thick and lemon-colored, about 5 minutes.
Gently fold in chocolate. Reheat slightly to melt chocolate, if
necessary. Stir in rum and vanilla.
Beat egg whites until foamy. Beat in 2 tablespoons sugar; beat until
stiff peaks form. Gently fold whites into chocolate-yolk mixture.
Pour into individual serving dishes. Chill at least 4 hours. Serve
with whipped cream, if desired. Makes 6 to 8 servings.

# cherry pudding cake
## *clafoutis*

This dish is typical peasant cooking for family meals in the Lomousin province during cherry season.

2 cups pitted black cherries,
   fresh, or 1 1-pound can Bing
   cherries, drained
2 tablespoons cognac or brandy
2 tablespoons sugar
1 cup milk
⅓ cup sugar
3 eggs
2 teaspoons vanilla
½ teaspoon almond extract
⅛ teaspoon salt
1 cup flour
Powdered sugar

Place cherries in small bowl; pour brandy over them. Stir in 2 tablespoons sugar; set aside.
In blender container place remaining ingredients, except powdered sugar, in order listed. Blend on high 1 minute, or beat all ingredients to form a smooth batter. Pour ¼ of batter into 9-inch pie pan (2 inches deep). Place in 350°F oven about 2 minutes, until batter is set. Place cherries on top of batter; add any cherry juice and remaining batter. Return to oven; continue to bake for 45 minutes, until a knife inserted in center can be withdrawn clean. Sprinkle cake generously with powdered sugar. Serve cake warm. Makes 6 to 8 servings.

# napoleons
## *mille-feuille*

½ recipe Puff Pastry (see Index) chilled
1 egg white, beaten
1 tablespoon water
1 recipe Pastry Cream (see Index)
2 cups powdered sugar
4 tablespoons milk or cream
1 square unsweetened chocolate
   melted with 2 teaspoons butter

Roll pastry into 14 × 8-inch rectangle, 3/8 thick. Prick dough thoroughly with fork. With pastry cutter cut into 16 pieces 3½ × 2 inches. Place dough on baking sheets covered with brown paper or 3 to 4 layers of paper towels. Chill dough ½ hour.
Mix egg white and water; brush over dough. Place in preheated 450°F oven 6 minutes. Reduce heat to 300°F; bake an additional 25 to 30 minutes, until lightly browned and crisp. Remove from pan; cool on wire rack. When cool, separate each pastry into 2 or 3 layers. Fill with Pastry Cream.
In small bowl beat powdered sugar and milk until smooth. Glaze tops with icing. Using pastry tube with straight tip filled with chocolate mixture, draw straight lines widthwise across glazed top of pastry at 1-inch intervals. Draw a toothpick through the chocolate lines at ½ inch intervals. Reverse the direction on alternate lines to form chevron pattern. Makes 16 pastries.

*crepes suzette*

# crepes suzette

6 sugar cubes
2 oranges
1 lemon
1 stick soft unsalted butter

¼ cup Grand Marnier curacao,
   Benedictine, or Cointreau
12 Dessert Crepes (see Index, Basic
   Crepes)
¼ cup brandy

Rub sugar cubes over rinds of oranges and lemon; combine with
butter. Place flavored butter in chafing dish; add juice of 1 orange
and 1 lemon and ¼ cup of one of above liqueurs. When contents
of pan are hot and bubbling, add crepes, one at a time. Coat each
crepe with sauce, fold it into a triangle, and push it to side of dish.
When all crepes are coated with sauce, arrange them over surface
of dish; allow them to heat through.
Flame the crepes with brandy. Serve immediately. Makes 6 servings.

# cherries jubilee
*cerises jubileé*

3 tablespoons red currant jelly
1 tablespoon butter
2 cups canned tart cherries, well-drained
½ cup kirsch
1 pint vanilla ice cream

Melt jelly in frypan. Add butter; stir until melted and hot. Add
cherries; heat through.
Heat kirsch in small saucepan. Pour over cherries, ignite with long
match, and let burn until flames die. Spoon hot cherries over ice
cream. Serve. Makes 4 servings.

 *picture on next page: cherries jubilee*

*cream horns*

# cream horns
*cornets*

½ recipe Puff Pastry
  (see Index), chilled
1 egg white
1 tablespoon water
Granulated sugar
1 recipe Pastry Cream
  (see Index)

½ cup heavy cream, whipped
  (optional)
Ground pistachio nuts and
  powdered sugar for garnish
  (optional)

Roll pastry into a 12 × 18-inch rectangle ⅛ inch thick. Cut 12 strips 1 inch wide and 10 inches long. This fits a cornet tube (available at gourmet and specialty shops) that is 4½ inches long. Starting at narrow end, wrap pastry around tube, overlapping rows by ¼ to ½ inch. Do not stretch dough. Press to seal ends. Place tubes 2 inches apart on baking sheets lined with brown paper or 3 to 4 layers of paper towels. Refrigerate dough ½ hour.
Bake dough in preheated 400°F oven 20 minutes.
Beat egg white and water.
Remove horns from oven and brush egg white on tops of horns. Sprinkle with granulated sugar. Return to oven. Bake an additional 5 minutes or until golden and glazed. Place on wire racks; cool slightly. Remove from tubes; cool completely.
Fold whipped cream into pastry cream; fill the horns. Garnish with nuts and powdered sugar if desired. Makes 12 horns.

*Note:* To make a cornet tube, use 2 layers of heavy-duty aluminum foil cut into a 9-inch square. Fold in half to make a triangle. Roll triangle into horn or cone shape 4½ inches long and 1½ inches wide at top. Fold foil edges to secure it.

61

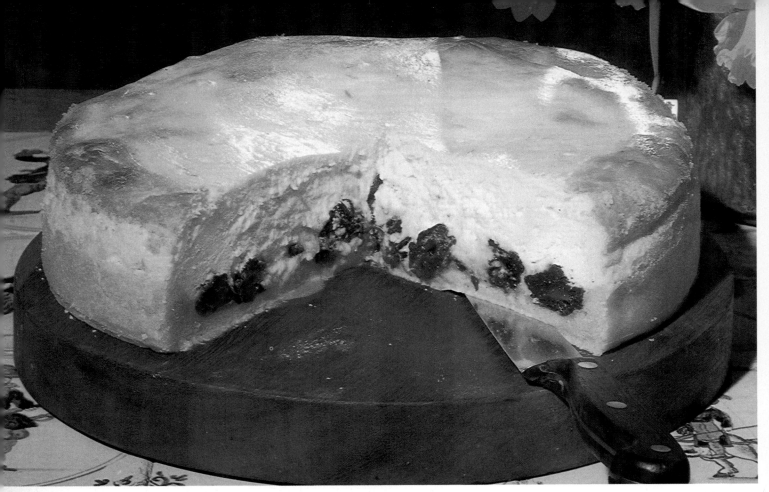

*cream-cheese tart with prunes*

# cream-cheese tart with prunes
## *tarte au fromage frais etaux pruneaux*

1 cup red wine
1½ cups water
1 piece cinnamon stick (about ¾ inch long)
4 whole cloves
¾ pound pitted prunes
1½ pounds cream cheese, softened
3 egg yolks
6 tablespoons cornstarch
1 cup heavy cream
4 tablespoons sugar
3 egg whites
1 teaspoon vanilla
Grated rind of ½ lemon
⅛ to ¼ cup powdered sugar
1 unbaked pie shell (see Index for Sweet Pastry Dough; place into 10-inch springform pan)

In medium saucepan combine red wine, water, cinnamon stick, cloves, and prunes. Bring to a boil; boil for 1 minute; simmer for 10 minutes. Set aside until ready to use.

In large bowl beat cream cheese, egg yolks, and cornstarch until light and fluffy. In separate bowl beat heavy cream until stiff; gradually add 3 tablespoons sugar.

In another bowl beat egg whites until stiff; beat in rest of sugar. Fold whipped cream, beaten egg whites, vanilla, and lemon rind carefully but thoroughly into cream-cheese mixture.

Drain prunes; discard cinnamon stick and cloves. Distribute over pie shell. Spread cream-cheese mixture over prunes. Smooth top with spatula. Bake in preheated 375°F oven 55 minutes. Remove tart from springform pan immediately after removing from oven. Let cool on cake rack. Sift a light coating of powdered sugar over top of tart. Makes 10 to 12 servings.

# index